HQ 1206 .W66 1991

Woo, Lillian C.

Women in change

DATE DUE

WITHDRAWN FROM THE EVAN'S
LIBRARY AT FMCC

**FULTON-MONTGOMERY COMMUNITY
COLLEGE LIBRARY**

WOMEN IN CHANGE

The Psychological Development
of American Women

Lillian C. Woo

CAROLINA ACADEMIC PRESS
DURHAM, NORTH CAROLINA

To Lillian Chung and the late Henry Chung, who, as parents, provided and supported a family environment of equal gender free expectations and opportunities for my brothers and me.

© Copyright 1991, Lillian C. Woo
All rights reserved

Library of Congress Card Catalog Number 91-75934
ISBN: 0-89089-477-9

Printed in the United States of America

Carolina Academic Press
700 Kent Street
Durham, N.C.
(919) 489-7486

Preface • vi

Acknowledgements • viii

Introduction • 3

Stage I: Hearth Tender • 8

Stage II: Superwoman • 21

Stage III: Beyond Superwoman • 48

From the Firing Line: A Case Study • 73

Stage IV: Boat Rocker • 83

Stage V: Grand Prix Winner • 104

Conclusion • 133

Notes • 136

Appendices • 140

References • 159

Index • 164

Preface

Since the publication of the *Feminine Mystique* and the birth of the women's movement more than three decades ago, the course and direction of the American woman's life has changed dramatically. Up to that point women were able to accomplish as much or as little as they chose without the world heralding each success or failure in the name of womanhood.

Since the 1960s we American women have not only been urged to fulfill ourselves but have also become fascinating research subjects. For almost 30 years we have been under a microscope to see what makes us tick. We have been probed, examined, and analyzed from every angle. Are we single children or one of many? Do we come from traditional families? Did we play team sports? Do we have a Cinderella complex, waiting for a prince to rescue us? Are we really afraid of success?

Just about every aspect of our lives and psychological background has been researched and documented. But the search goes on to find out even more about why we behave the way we do and what behavior and traits we must have in order to succeed.

The large body of accumulated scholarly research has been very distinguished and important. It has examined a wide range of background characteristics and female behavior which influence our lives. Studies about depression, anxiety, self-esteem, success, and androgyny have added a great deal to our knowledge and understanding of women, and more subjects are being probed every day.

There is no doubt that in the last 30 years we have been the subject of many intriguing theories about our problems which have resulted from the American social structure and value systems. Some of the complex, insufficient parental encouragement, and the gender inferiority complex.

The media has added to this endless interest in our behavior by generating public discussions and forums about each theory and problem and by increasing women's awareness of their traditions and potential.

However, it is important for us women to keep a level head about new breakthroughs which explain why we do what we do and how we became the women we are. The breadth and depth of scholarly work on the many and different facets of a woman's life, and the press' eagerness to report major new discoveries about American women have created a public pressure which makes it almost impossible for us not to get caught up in the latest explanations of our successes and failures. As good and valid as the research and studies are, we need to keep in mind that the research and theories do not apply to *all* women in general, just segments of us.

Even though most of us have been exposed to roughly the same traditions and culture, we actually represent many different stages of psychological development. Each particular stage of development has its own set of behavior and attitudes, strengths and weaknesses, rational and irrational beliefs, limitations and potentials. We simply cannot be lumped into one universal category. To do so can and does cause confusion.

That is why I wrote *Women in Change*. It is an attempt to explain the complexities of the American woman using a new set of hypotheses and a new approach. This book hopes to shed some light on the psychological stages of development using new as well as past research, theories, and studies.

While life would be much simpler if all women could be categorized as "just like a woman," the fact is that we are all different. This fact makes it hard, if not impossible, to generalize about female behavior and value systems. Some women suffer from fear of success, but many do not. Some women seek out assertiveness training, but most don't. Some women are in an evolutionary process, but a very large number are not. Some women need support groups, but many have done a great deal on their own.

The primary purpose of this book is to help all of us understand ourselves a little better and to encourage all women to move psychologically beyond their present stage if we choose to do so.

ACKNOWLEDGEMENTS

My great appreciation and thanks go to the following people whose guidance, expertise, suggestions, and support were invaluable: William Self and Julio George at the University of North Carolina for recognizing the need and establishing the Center for Women in Educational Leadership, the goal of which is to identify and train women for top management, and for their strong support of the CWEL program; Martha McKay, founder of the North Carolina Women's Political Caucus and the North Carolina Women's Forum, for providing women with strength, through example and encouragement, to aspire and achieve; Dr. Vivian Travis, professor of psychology and consultant to CWEL, for patiently and generously sharing her considerable knowledge, experience, and insights on the psychology of women, for being my mentor in feminine psychology, and for guiding the formulation of the book's focus; the late Ivan Hill whose great wisdom, kindness, and lifelong dedication to ethics had an emboldening influence on both my own personal growth and on the spirit and direction of the book; Dollie Smith, Dwayne Walls, Jane Woo, and Beadsie Woo, whose reviews of and comments on the manuscript I value almost as much as their friendship; the wonderful women who were interviewed for the book for their generous willingness to share their life experiences so that all women may benefit from them.

WOMEN IN CHANGE

INTRODUCTION

For the past 30 years, millions of women have charted a course which has included a career as well as a home, rigorous competition in business as well as family security. Millions of us have stepped forward to fulfill ourselves and to claim our own successes.

This movement has had a profound effect. It has freed many women from the traditions and limitations which kept our mothers bound. It has made us more aware of our talents and possibilities and given us many more opportunities and choices professionally and personally. It has made possible greater freedoms, greater aspirations, and far greater achievements. But it has also produced many more internal conflicts.

Despite the women's movement and its heralded "emancipation," there are also millions of us who have been content to maintain the status quo. Some of us have no desire to change either ourselves or the system.

The status quo camp and the women's movement camp have become vocal critics of each other's lifestyles, attitudes, behavior, and values. Each group thinks that it is right. Neither will give in. To concede anything worthwhile in the opponent's camp would be considered a betrayal of one's own life course.

The attempt to ratify the Equal Rights Amendment was the main battlefield for a long time. In that arena, the lines were drawn fiercely and distinctly. The anti-ERA group accused ERA supporters of advocating the dissolution of the American family. By rushing out to work and by not staying home to take care of their children, these pro-ERA women, their detractors alleged, were destroying the foundation of American society and the core of the family. Retaliating in equally harsh terms, the ERA supporters charged that the anti-ERA women were walking anachronisms with unrealistic fantasies about being princesses and being taken care of by men. These child/women would never reach their personhood because they wanted to be dependent and adored rather than independent and self-actualized.

Although ERA is no longer a hot issue, the struggle between the two groups shows no sign of letting up.

Those who have elected to maintain their traditional roles have been made to feel very inadequate by those women who have chosen a full-time career track. Those who have elected to be full-time homemakers have been made to feel very inadequate by those mothers who have outside jobs and professions.

On the other hand, women who have succeeded away from the hearth have also been subjected to criticism. If a woman is physically attractive, the traditionalists often accuse her of flirting or sleeping her way to the top. If a woman is plain, detractors call her a "bitch" and say that she needs a "good man" to keep her straight.

The world at large, however, has taken up the flag of the working woman and ignored the millions who have chosen to retain a traditional woman's role.

There is no doubt that the path to a greater fulfillment for women has been far from smooth. In fact, it has been lined with obstacles, problems, barriers, and conflicts.

The new juggling act which women have undertaken has become the focus of both academic analysis and practical advice. There has been a constant flood of material in scholarly and popular journals on a mind-boggling array of topics: handling job and family, job discrimination, unequal treatment, organizational dynamics, corporate politics, support systems, motivation, power, dressing for success, managerial styles, and many other issues.

These subjects are valid and often apply to tens of thousands of women, and many have provided assistance to women in tapping their potential and meeting challenges. However, while these analyses and advice have benefited many women, it has been useless to others. Some women don't want to change, some are afraid to change, and others have moved beyond the level of advice being offered.

But the overwhelming volume of self-help information and reaffirming support may have not only increased awareness but also caused confusion and overload. This wide proliferation of literature and advice has actually created a global guilt in most women. Each woman can accept or reject one or two articles on these subjects, but the unrelenting plethora of these articles can eventually wear down anyone's resistance and self-confidence. At some point each woman begins to think that perhaps something is wrong with her if she doesn't personally have these problems that everyone seems to want to help her solve.

For women to select their own directions and to avoid massive social pressures to conform to a life and value system they may not want, they must first try to find out where they are in their psychological development. After that, they can decide what to do next.

In *Women In Change*, I identify and discuss five stages of psychological development in women: Stage I Hearth Tender, Stage II Superwoman, Stage III Beyond Superwoman, Stage IV Boat Rocker, and Stage V Grand Prix Winner.

Stage I: Hearth Tender. This woman accepts the tradition of sugar and spice and everything nice. She believes that the prince will rescue her and they will ride off into the sunset together and live happily ever after.

Hearth Tender is totally satisfied with her status. She is not aware of any special problems either she or other women encounter in the world. She lacks self-initiation and is not interested in going out into the world to accomplish something herself. In other words, she has no desire to change herself or the system.

She believes in the "natural law" of male dominance. She limits her role to minor and structured tasks. She is not a leader.

But she can be manipulative and deceptive. She uses her feminine wiles to get what she wants and has mastered the art of helplessness. Because she uses such indirect methods to get what she wants, she is completely powerless. This results in a very poor self-image. But since she is unaware of who she is and where she is, she is satisfied with her psychological stage and makes no effort to move beyond it.

Stage II: Superwoman. This woman has some awareness of her status and the special problems of women in leadership roles. Many Superwomen are in the job market but deliberately limit their own growth professionally. They complain about the unfairness of their positions but rarely see the need to change themselves or others.

Superwoman's leadership potential is limited and restricted. She leads a life which is determined by others, not herself. She tries to please everyone and tries to avoid conflict by simply doing everything. She feels that if she fills all the roles, as a Superwoman, she can escape criticism and conflict. She feels that she will be fulfilled if she gears her life and skills to helping others.

The Stage II woman suffers from fear of success. She is not interested in exercising power or getting too far up the career ladder. She always chooses personal relationships over power, so she is likely to turn down promotions that separate her from her friends.

She also suffers from guilt and depression because she is not assertive. She denies her own needs and truly believes that everything will be all right if she concentrates on serving others. She avoids confrontation at all costs, and as a result, is totally powerless. Because she knows that she is powerless, she tries to get others to like her by doing everything they want. She never stops trying.

Stage III: Beyond Superwoman. This woman is not fully satisfied with the status she inherited and has taken steps to develop special coping skills. She has a great deal of awareness of the special problems she and other women encounter. She has moved beyond Superwoman, but she has developed her own set of coping skills. She has found "what works for me" and is content with that. She has no special interest in formal training in management skills, no need for support groups, and very little desire to change the system. She has done everything on her own. She has achieved a degree of leadership and power and feels comfortable with the success she has gained so far. She does not particularly want to go beyond her achieved level of success or power. She prides herself on her ability to get along with others and attributes her success to this trait rather than to her skills.

Stage IV: Boat Rocker. This woman is not at all satisfied with her status and actively seeks out training to overcome the problems she perceives to be particular to women in leadership roles. She forms support systems and actively works to change herself and the system. She welcomes opportunities to learn about power issues, managerial styles, and organizational politics. She seeks out leadership roles and does no back away from conflict. She is assertive and speaks her mind openly and honestly at home and at work. Because of this, she takes a lot of heat and receives a great deal of negative feedback from rocking the boat.

She does not fear success; rather, she continually looks for new levels of it. Her positive and negative experiences enable her to grow stronger and more determined. She is usually quite successful in her personal relationships because she is self-assured and comfortable with her own identity.

Stage V: Grand Prix Winner. Grand Prix Winners have resolved most of the conflicts and issues they faced in their lives. They have been on the front lines and labored at changing themselves and the system. They initiate change and have reached a high level of self-actualization. Grand Prix Winners have successfully adapted themselves psychologically to the changing role of women and feel comfortable with their successes and their exercise of power. They have a firm sense of self-worth and have progressed beyond the Cinderella complex, fear of success, guilt, and denial.

She does not feel threatened by others, is capable of being tender and generous toward others because they feel comfortable about their own femininity, identity, capability, and status. They are realistic about what they can do and the kinds of impact they can have. There aren't very many of these women.

These five stages are designed to be a general guide to the parameters of psychological growth. They are in no way meant to simplistically categorize women into stages. There is no magic age or profession that places a woman in one stage over another. Only her psychological development determines her present stage. Most women, in fact, do not fit into any one category entirely. Most straddle stages, and during their lifetime many will continue to refine the dynamic of psychological adaptation to keep up with the changes of society. This continuum of change can and will benefit all women. From Hearth Tender to Grand Prix Winner, women can search for growth and fulfillment of their time, purpose, and a satisfied sense of being.

Some women arrive at a point where they feel most comfortable. Many remain uncomfortable for most of their lives, some by choice and others because they will not stretch themselves and take risks in the area of human growth. No matter where a woman begins and no matter where she finally ends, she can find contentment, challenge, and happiness as long as she knows where she is and chooses to be there.

Stage I: Hearth Tender

The American woman has been molded by society's perception of who she is, what she represents, and the role she fills. Society has decided that the American woman represents everything good about this country.

The term "as American as motherhood and apple pie" says it all. What the American woman has come to symbolize in our society is almost as important to the development and prosperity of the United States as democracy, freedom, and free enterprise. She has become the backbone of the social stability which has allowed this country to prosper and develop.

This powerful image of the traditional American woman has been used to represent the country's ideals and dreams in war, in peace, in economic recessions, in prosperity—in its broadest representational sense and its personal emotional sense. She has become the symbol of the national goodness. She has kept the home fire burning; she has been the cohesive force in the family; she is the primary source of warmth and love. She is the woman we remember from so many Norman Rockwell paintings: a woman wearing an apron, holding a plate of cookies and a pitcher of lemonade on the back porch as her children run up the walkway after school.

That picture lives in our hearts and memories and takes on the mythic proportions of an ideal. And although we know cognitively that this image is a highly romanticized vision of perfection, society nevertheless has set standards for and expectations of its "all-American" woman. Many, many women today live their lives trying to fulfill those expectations. They are the Hearth Tenders.

Martha is a typical Hearth Tender. The only daughter of a well-to-do farmer, Martha was raised as her father's "Little Princess" and was given every opportunity and privilege: ballet lessons, horseback riding, piano lessons, cotillion classes, summers at the beach or in Europe.

Her parents and grandparents doted on her and couldn't do enough for her. "Mama and Daddy wanted to be sure that I grew up with all the proper skills and the culture of a fine lady," Martha admits. "They let me associate only with people they felt were socially acceptable."

After high school Martha went to a two-year women's college where she polished her social skills, learned a little about music and art history, and met the "right" kind of men—all in the finishing school tradition. So, at the age of twenty, Martha represented the quintessence of the well-bred young woman. Soft-spoken, immaculately groomed with the perfect posture of a beauty queen, she could get anything she wanted just by smiling and asking for it in her well-rehearsed breathy voice.

She returned home after college and immediately became the toast of local society. She married the most eligible bachelor in town within a year of her return and moved into a large, comfortable home, just ten miles from where she was born.

Martha settled into the life she had been preparing for. She became the most sought-after young hostess and community leader in the area. Her home and family were the models for everyone in that part of the state. Now, thirty-five years later, Martha is still doing all the community projects, fundraisers, charity balls, and political campaigns which are socially acceptable. She has been the president of every organization in her county and area of the state.

She has distinguished herself as an indefatigable worker, a constant ray of sunshine and source of joy, and a good team member. Martha has relished these many roles.

Martha's style of operating always ensures that she will come out ahead. Here is an example: As the presiding chairman of a regional meeting, Martha encountered some unexpected hostility. A faction leader questioned one of her decisions and the process of selecting nominees for particular offices. It was quite obvious that the entire delegation was sympathetic with the faction leader and demanded to hear an explanation. Martha, under fire, at the age of 55, defended herself as she had done her entire life: she batted her eyes, spoke haltingly in a breathy voice as if to fight back tears, stroked her neck in a semiseductive way, and assumed the role of the helpless little girl. Although her explanation was not satisfactory, Martha succeeded in eliciting sympathy for her point of view. Her "poor little me"[1] act had worked that day as it had worked during her entire life.

Martha has made a whole career out of this traditional passive behavior, and obviously she is very satisfied with the results. She has successfully adapted to the system in which she was born and has absolutely no wish to change it. She has achieved status, popularity, and a degree of leadership using her own style. Why change a good thing?

Martha acquired her style through her mother, grandmother, and all the preceding generations. Women in her family had been raised to be helpless and dependent in the grand tradition of Scarlett O'Hara. This kind of sociologically nostalgic behavior is very strong and is handed down like an heirloom from one generation to another.

Although Martha is from the South and represents many women from the region, the Hearth Tender is found everywhere in the country because she is truly the traditional American woman.

The traditional American woman has always been coddled and protected from the harsh world of hard knocks. From childhood girls are discouraged from rigorous, competitive activities and are rewarded instead for being helpful and sweet.

Harvard professor Carol Gilligan reinforces this tradition in her book *In a Different Voice*. She asserts that women are typically different from men in their orientations toward life because these orientations are formed early and irreversibly through a child's relationship with its mother.[2]

Girls are taken care of by their parents, their teachers, their relatives, and ultimately their husbands. They're treated like fairy tale princesses during their formative years and consequently never develop coping skills or a strong sense of self-esteem. As they grow up, then, women use affiliation and affection toward others to survive. They have never struck out on their own and therefore have never acquired a sense of independence or self-confidence. They didn't have to; their parents did everything for them.

These parents did not deliberately raise their daughters to be helpless, vulnerable underachievers. They were just conscientiously following the advice of childhood experts. But the results were to create adults who were unable to survive on their own. Conversely, girls whose mothers did not hover and cater to their children turned out to be high achievers.

In their book, *Beyond Sugar and Spice*,[3] Caryl Rivers, Rosalind Barnett, and Grace Baruch document research on early childhood development differences between boys and girls. The authors indicate that boys at as early as age six have a tendency to overestimate both their abilities as well as their prospects for success. On the other hand, girls show just the opposite attitudes.

A study of fifth graders by Carol Dweck and Ellen Bush at the University of Illinois showed that teachers give negative feedback equally to boys and girls, but boys are criticized more often for behavior problems than for the quality of their school work. The girls received criticism mostly for their school work.

In that study teachers felt that the boys had the ability to do the work but lacked motivation. On the other hand, they felt that girls did not have the ability to do the work.[4]

With this type of socialization from an early age, boys and girls develop behavior and attitudes which respond to and underscore the world's preconceived ideas about them:

• Boys tend to overestimate their skills and future success. Girls tend to underestimate their abilities.

• Boys accept success because they have confidence in their abilities; girls attribute their success to external factors, such as luck or circumstances rather than to skills.

• Boys who fail rationalize that they didn't try hard enough. Girls who fail feel that they are not competent or intelligent enough.

An extensive study of male and female stereotypes was conducted by Broverman and his colleagues.[5] The results of this study showed that the influence of traditional sex roles is so great that men and women get locked into them very easily. Women become conditioned to suppress anger, to be nonassertive about their opinions and preferences, and to be passive followers rather than leaders. Men, on the other hand, have been conditioned to be stoic and brave at all times. It is unthinkable for a man to cry, physically touch another man, express personal fears, or admit weaknesses. As a result of these sex typed roles, women have a reputation for tact and sensitivity toward others, and men are regarded as more independent and objective.

Developmental psychologist Sandra Bem has also done research on the psychology of sex roles based on adult self-definitions of feminine and masculine traits. It is based on her idea that coping in modern society requires adults to be assertive, independent, and self-reliant as well as sensitive and caring. But traditional views of male and female traits seem to preclude male traits in women and female traits in men.

Bem's famous sex role inventory was first introduced in 1970. Specific masculine traits were selected by a large sample of undergraduates to be more desirable for a man than for a woman, and specific female traits were thought to be more desirable for a woman than for a man.[5]

Masuline Items

Acts as a leader
Aggressive
Ambitious
Analytical
Athletic
Competitive
Defends own beliefs
Dominant
Forceful
Has leadership abilities

Independent
Individualistic
Makes decisions easily
Masculine
Self-reliant
Self-sufficient
Strong personality
Willing to take a stand
Willing to take risks

Feminine Items

Affectionate
Cheerful
Childlike
Compassionate
Does not use harsh language
Eager to soothe
  hurt feelings
Feminine
Flatterable
Gentle
Gullible

Loves children
Loyal
Sensitive to other's needs
Shy
Soft-spoken
Sympathetic
Tender
Understanding
Warm
Yielding

Neutral Items

Adaptable
Conceited
Conscientious
Conventional
Friendly
Happy
Helpful
Inefficient
Jealous
Likeable

Moody
Reliable
Secretive
Sincere
Solemn
Tactful
Theatrical
Truthful
Unpredictable
Unsystematic

From this list, it is clear that women are more sensitive and nurturing and men tend to have more leadership and competitive qualities. The Hearth Tender has all of the feminine characteristics and none of the masculine ones. The Hearth Tender falls into the category Sandra Bem calls the feminine woman.[7] She never has had the need to develop masculine traits or to become androgynous and in traditional households was discouraged from doing so. All that was expected of young Hearth Tenders was to be sweet, loveable, and helpful.

If a woman is socialized from birth to underrate herself and to develop only one set of coping skills, she never has a chance to become anything but a Hearth Tender.

Martha grew up with the security of her family's financial success, the security of a finishing school, and the security of her limited universe of activities and people. Traditional women like Martha never received encouragement to strike out on their own or to develop independence. They almost never face the challenges of the outside world because they have been protected at every juncture in their lives.

Martha and other traditional women are satisfied with their status and role in life. They grew up in an environment where all their needs were taken care of, and when they were old enough, a prince arrived to rescue them. They were carried off into the sunset to a palace of their own.

Martha thrives on her status and leadership roles. "I just love people. I want to help in any way that I can to make things better. I've been around so long it finally was my turn to be president of this or chairman of that. I've been blessed with an easy life and have been very lucky too."

Typical of a Hearth Tender, Martha attributes her success to luck and persistence. She explains her activities and satisfaction in terms of nurturing and helping others. She never mentions her abilities and skills, because she thinks they are limited. Her statement of modesty reflects more a lack of self-confidence than humility.

In her book *Women and Anxiety* psychiatrist Helen DeRosis reports that over 50 percent of her patients correspond to the Hearth Tender.[8] They are dependent women with low self-esteem. These women find comfort in living their lives as they always have. The predictability of each day helps maintain an important equilibrium in their lives. Like Martha, the Hearth Tenders have the same lifestyle and attitudes today as they had while growing up.

Hearth Tenders buy into the system of prescribed behavior. They exchange their independence for being taken care of. They willingly perpetuate their bondage to a myth.[9]

Hearth Tenders are satisfied with the status they inherited. They do not want to set the world on fire. They do not want to achieve very much. Consequently, they limit their roles.

Marthas's leadership, for example, has been largely confined to areas which are traditionally female: church women's guild, junior women's clubs, garden club, art society, cancer society. She is content to assume these socially acceptable roles. They don't threaten her view of the natural order of male supremacy.

Hearth Tenders feel that males are naturally superior. They feel that men and their activities are more important than those of women. And traditional males perpetuate this notion.

Consider Walter, 57, a mainline Philadelphian whose family had been part of the original settlers of the city. His family spent summers at Cape Cod as many affluent city families did and still do. He attended a prestigious prep school and an elite men's college. When it was considered an activity which only the wealthy could afford, Walter would spend his college spring vacations basking in the Bahamas.

It is clear from this description that Walter and his family have always felt that their destiny is to be leaders. He was raised to exert his authority both in the corporate world and in the family.

Right after college Walter got married, did his stint in the army, and then joined the corporate ranks with his goal of becoming chief executive officer and chairman of the board of one of the Fortune 500 companies. Here he perfected his ability to be decisive and authoritative.

He was the same way at home. Walter was the undisputed rule of the roost. He brought up his daughters to get married and have a family. It was unthinkable that his daughters would work outside the home after they had children. It was the responsibility of their husbands to provide an adequate quality of life for his daughters.

"I think that this whole women's movement has really decreased the quality of life for women. It isn't her job to get out there and help support the family. Her husband should be able to support her."

Asked if he thought that women should be treated equally, Walter replied, "Of course. As the father of three daughters, I want them to have equal opportunity in everything they do. Just because I believe in a clear delineation of roles is no reason to think that I advocate the subordination of women to men.

"I was brought up to believe than men supported the family and women raised the children, took care of the home, and did good deeds in the community. My grandparents lived like that, my parents followed in their footsteps, and my wife and I have had a very happy arrangement for over 30 years.

"Although she was trained as a nurse, my wife never worked in her profession. We started our family right away, and she devoted all her time to the family. Personally, I am very proud of the way the girls turned out, and I attribute it to two things: (1) my wife stayed home and gave them the love and encouragement they needed, and (2) our family had stability through clear roles for everybody."

To Walter and millions of men, the family is a paradigm of what American tradition is all about—in its stability, its strength, its propriety and integrity, its proud heritage and splendid preservation. As a result, this value system and its moral principles, as part of a continuing family legacy, are transmitted from the past to the future with great conviction, passion, and a sense of rightness.

If Hearth Tenders grow up with fathers like Walter, they acquire a value system which attributes greater power and intellectual judgment to men. From childhood on, they observe that women do not venture into the outside work world and do not develop as much savvy or knowledge as men.

Martha believes that men are smarter and more capable than women. Asked by friends and political activists to run for public offfice, Martha declined. "I don't know how to wheel and deal power. The issues are too complicated. What if I made a mistake? A man should hold the job," she explained.

This statement reveals a lot about Martha's views of herself. First she puts herself down by saying she is not smart enough to grasp either the issues or the political maneuvering. In reality, though, Martha has proven that she is quite adept in her club work and always manages to establish good working relationships with others. In her sphere, she is a capable leader and more than likely can be very effective in public office. But she lacks the self-confidence to go beyond her own self-imposed universe. In her mind, and in the minds of all Hearth Tenders, her activities are not as important as anything a man does, so she disparages her own accomplishments and successes.

Martha accepts the social definition of reality for women to nurture others and help them fulfill their goals.

Second, she doesn't have enough self-esteem to expand her psychological boundaries. She prefers to remain within the confines of a secure world where all the rules are known and where personal affiliations are comfortable. As a result, Martha will never be able to take risks and opportunities which might result in personal growth. She wants to stay the way she is, and the world she has set up for herself ensures that.

Third, she believes that men should be in charge, and women should be their helpers. It never occurred to her that women may have the talent and strength to be leaders. Her mental stereotype and tradition of both female roles and female behavior are so strong, she has never even thought about behaving in any other way.

Anne Wilson Schaef in her book *Women's Reality*[10] would classify Martha and other Hearth Tenders as products of the original sin-- being born female. Schaef's hypothesis reinforces the major characteristics and behavior of Hearth Tenders: (1) These women feel that they are innately inferior to men. (2) These women feel that they are not complete or whole unless there is a connection with other people and most importantly with a man. (3) These women have poor self-esteem and constantly need approval and validation from men. Validation and praise from other women don't count, because Hearth Tenders distrust other women and feel that compliments from them don't mean very much. (4) These women seek a protected existence in which everything proceeds according to an invisible and utopian plan. (5) These women do not want to take risks or assume positions of perceived power. This is counter to the "way it should be"—with men in charge and women as followers. (6) These women attack and put down other women because they think that they don't depend on other women for their identity. Criticism of other women soothes the Hearth Tender because she wants to believe that others are not as good as she is. This pecking order mentality does not, in fact, provide a psychological boost to the Hearth Tender. Rather, it confirms the Hearth Tender's subconscious view of herself. She doesn't really like herself.

Although Hearth Tenders seem to lead a placid and secure existence and say that they're content and happy, some are actually very depressed without knowing it. Experts in the field of female depression like Helen DeRosis have found that poor self-esteem is a prime cause of depression among women. This depression is especially prevalent among Hearth Tenders.

The protective parents of Hearth Tenders unwittingly produced poor self-images in their daughters. By doing everything for their daughters, by giving them every advantage and specialty lessons, these parents thought they were being good parents. Instead of transmitting love, care, and security to their daughters, these parents were actually sending a strong message that "you are not acceptable as you are, and we are making every effort to improve you."[11]

This unintended message of inadequacy conveyed from parent to daughter leads ultimately to her lack of self-confidence. According to DeRosis in *Women and Anxiety*, this woman cannot accept herself as she is. She has constant feelings that she is never quite good enough in anything she does as a worker, parent, spouse, or friend. Consequently, she is driven by an obsession to live up to an ideal image so that she will feel more worthy.[12]

This image, which deprives her of a free choice in dealing with herself and others, was first identified in women in the 1930s by psychiatrist Karen Horney. To this day, it shows no sign of relinquishing its tyrannical hold on millions of American women: "loving" mothers should and must always care for their families; "helpful" wives must always be cheerful and supportive of their husbands and must be good helpers; "conscientious" workers must always perform any task they are asked to do; and "nice" women don't ever get angry.

What happens to a woman who has low self-esteem and is also driven by this fictitious image of a good woman? She becomes overwhelmed by the system and by a feeling of helplessness. She becomes depressed because she is struggling with feelings of inferiority, guilt, and fear.[13]

Most Hearth Tenders cope with their depression through denial. This is a very common survival technique. They subconsciously deny that they ever fall short of their goals or the image they estabished for themselves. They consciously rationalize their shortcomings and explain at length the reasons for actions and views which they perceive to be unacceptable. They practice massive self-deception; they are never able to distinguish between fact and fantasy, and they have a hard time accepting anything less than perfection.

Blanche, 34, is another typical Hearth Tender. A bouncy blonde who still looks like a college cheerleader, Blanche works as a manager in a very large corporation. She is bright and capable. She does an excellent job in that position. In addition, her personality is always bright and happy. She cracks jokes, compliments people to make them feel good, brings homemade cookies to the office, and generally is well liked by everyone in the department.

But Blanche doesn't feel that this job is her real purpose in life. After her husband Jake died, she and her two children were left on their on. She is working to support herself and the children, but she feels that her real mission in life is to find a man who will marry her and take over this responsibility. She then will be able to stay home again and do the needlepointing and interior decorating she loves.

After a day at the office, Blanche opens cans of soup for the children's dinner, since she is too tired to do any other cooking. Sometimes she goes out with women friends to the movies or the shopping center. However, if a man asks her for a date, she will immediately cancel any plans she has with women friends. She feels that keeping company with women is a last resort, only if no man has asked her out.

When she is dating a man, her entire life changes. She cooks gourmet meals and redecorates her apartment to match his taste. She buys clothes that she thinks he likes. She turns herself upside down to please him. And while this is going on, she never calls her women friends. This cycle has repeated itself endlessly for the last four years, and there is no end in sight.

Because Blanche is preoccupied with a permanent affiliation with a man, she has neglected her own development. She still functions well on her own, but she never reads, she never travels, she never goes to any civic events. She just waits for the phone to ring. It might be Mr. Right.

Blanche provides an extreme example for her children about appropriate adult behavior. They are growing up in an environment where a succession of men are paraded through the apartment for varying lengths of time. They are given time only when Blanche doesn't have a date. They undoubtedly have the feeling that they are not as important to their mother as a male stranger. They are growing up without enough psychological and emotional support for them to become confident, secure adults.

"Oh, yeah, I get down sometimes. But I keep so busy that I don't think about it," Blanche admits when asked whether she is ever depressed. "But when I start dating a new man, I am on cloud nine, and I know that everything is going to turn out okay.

"I think my children understand that sometimes I can't give them as much attention as I would like because all of us want to have a daddy around again. And that is a top priority for the children and me."

Blanche can be classified as a love-addicted woman. Her identity is determined through acknowledgement and affirmation she receives from another person, usually a man. She has no identity of her own; that is why she takes on the characteristics of a chameleon in her apartment and in her dress to match her latest paramour's taste.

According to DeRosis the most important things in a love-addicted woman's life are love and serving others. Her self-esteem depends totally on being affirmed by others. She thinks that she has to have a partner and a sense of unity with that partner before she can find the meaning of life. She cannot enjoy doing anything by herself; she cannot express anger or criticism without feeling guilty. And when she is sad, she expects Brownie points for her suffering.[4]

Women like Blanche are normally attracted to a man who seems strong and superior, but this man is usually neurotic and treats Blanche like dirt. This kind of treatment confirms what Blanche already thinks of herself: she really doesn't like the person she is.

Stanley was a typical example of a man Blanche dates. Blanche dated Stanley, who was by his own admission a lady's man. But Blanche didn't care. When she was with Stan everything in the world was rose-colored. It didn't matter that Stan was also dating six other women whom he described as "sluts." He came to see Blanche whenever he felt like it; he took advantage of her in every way. He wasn't even nice. But Blanche didn't mind. She was so pleased that he would take her out. She didn't even worry about contracting any sexually transmitted disease from this multi-partnered relationship. The affiliation with Stan was all that mattered.

At the rate Blanche is going, she will continue to be seduced sexually and emotionally by any man who makes her feel accepted She will continue to run as fast as she can on this love track until the day that she acknowledges her true feelings and comes to grips with her sense of selfhood, her conflicts, and reality.

The prospects of Blanche's changing her lifestyle and attitudes are relatively slim. Hearth Tenders generally are passive and helpless. They don't make things happen that would alter their lives. Socialized to be protected, the Hearth Tender has spun a psychological cocoon around herself so that she will be sufficiently insulated and can then function and get a degree of satisfaction from her life.

Within the confines of that insulated world, the Hearth Tender remains quite childlike throughout her life. She never grows away from dependency and helplessness. She never develops healthy self-confidence. The origins of these traits have been discussed earlier, so it is clear that the Hearth Tender is more the product of overprotection than neglect, too much love rather than abuse.

This paradox between intent and result has created millions of Hearth Tenders in this country, and because these traits have been perpetuated for over a hundred years, the Hearth Tender became the symbol of American motherhood, the symbol of family strength. The Hearth Tender is alive and well today, despite the pressures of the past three decades for women to become more liberated and equal. By and large, Hearth Tenders have remained unaffected. They don't seem to be aware of the problems women encounter in society and the workplace, and if they do know about these obstacles facing women, they dismiss them because these barriers don't apply to their lives.

Although Hearth Tenders win some small battles, they never win the war. They continue to deal with the small problems over and over again, because they have never examined their true feelings or developed honest, open communication with others. The result of this lifetime of deceptive maneuvering is devastating for the Hearth Tender.

The lack of self-esteem, the depression, the inability to have total satisfaction, the helplessness and powerlessness all go unnoticed by the Hearth Tender. And that is perhaps the only way she can survive. She is oblivious to either her psychological or emotional state and is unaffected by the women's movement. She has minimal mental and emotional conflict about her values and behavior because she is unaware of any other systems.

There is no doubt that the Hearth Tender has played an important role in the formation of society as America developed. And she continues to thrive in very large numbers. To the extent that she feels satisfied with her life and her contribution to her community and family, the Hearth Tender is an integral part of the social fabric of this country. The Hearth Tender should take proper credit for her efforts and skills which have benefitted so many causes and helped progress. The stability she has provided is invaluable.

In a socially complex time in which many women are searching for new roles and men are learning to adapt to these changes, the Hearth Tender may seem almost anachronistic. But the overriding fact is that the Hearth Tender is satisfied with her life. That is more than some woman at other stages can claim.

Hearth Tenders represent a simpler existence and relatively satisfactory one.

STAGE II: SUPERWOMAN

We all know the old saying, "Never underestimate the power of a woman." Just what does that mean? What kind of power is it—physical, mental, emotional? Does it imply that women are powerful and influential even though their physical frames may be petite? Does it suggest that women are devious and cunning in getting what they want? The ambiguity of that saying leaves much to individual interpretation and, I believe, adds more social mystery to women.

The kind of power women wielded certainly has changed as times have changed. The definition and forms of power have also changed as women and men altered their relationships with each other and changed their professional and personal emphases and goals.

Socialization and advertising are two of the primary influences that created Superwoman from Hearth Tender.

In a world which has become overrun by superlatives, there can no longer be anything plain or ordinary. Hence, the terms *superstar*, *megabuck*, and *superwoman*. Superwoman was coined to describe the modern woman, the woman with verve and flair, the woman with a sense of adventure, the woman who will no longer settle for the lifestyle and values of her mother and grandmother. Superwoman wants to do it all--have a career, family, and an equal chance to do whatever she wants.

While there is, in fact, no such person as a Superwoman, advertising and the growth of the women's movement generated pressures to distinguish between old and new value systems, between "modern" and traditional women. And somewhere in the plethora of literature on "modern" women, the term *Superwoman* was created.

This chapter addresses itself to a discussion of women who are in Stage II of psychological development. The term *Superwoman* is used for this stage because these women try to do everything and fill many roles as: career woman, mother, wife, gourmet cook, interior decorator, sports woman, fashion plate, sex symbol, civic leader, and elegant hostess. Only a Superwoman could do all that.

These activities and mindset are major departures from the simpler, socially sanctioned activities of the Hearth Tender. They don't represent a logical evolution of the role of women, but a more radical revolution against conventional values and behavior.

What were the catalysts which encouraged women to abandon the old and seek out the new? What made women decide that being a Hearth Tender was stifling? Let's look at the origins of Superwoman.

Origins. The most important influence on anyone is socialization. Socialization refers to the pressures—rewards, punishments, criticism, praise—which push a child toward conforming to "acceptable" responses. These responses are standards of behavior which society has set as the accepted norm, and since most parents want their children to blend in rather than to be "oddballs" in society, they mold their children's behavior from infancy on.

Judith Bardwick has researched extensively the socialization process and its effects on adults. In an article she coauthored with Elizabeth Douvan, Bardwick points out that girls are less active physically, display less overt physical aggression, and are more sensitive to physical pain. On the other hand, they show much greater verbal, perceptual, and cognitive skills. As a result, girls are better than boys at analyzing and anticipate adult demands and conform their behavior to adult expectations.

Boys are more physically and emotionally impulsive, are more prone to act out aggression, and are less well developed in cognitive and perceptive skills.

Bardwick and Douvan also state that dependent behavior in young boys is prohibited by social standards, but is permitted in young girls. The long-term result, then, is that girls are not encouraged to give up their old techniques of relating to adults and using other people to define their identity, to manipulate the physical world, and to supply their emotional needs.[1]

Raised in an environment with these values and socialization, young girls become women who remain dependent on other people's acceptance and love. They continue to use the skills of others instead of developing their own. Neither the girl's characteristic responses nor widespread cultural values force her to give up older, successful modes of relating and coping when she becomes a woman.

Adolescent females learn to emphasize the use of a cosmetic

exterior of self to lure men and to secure acceptance and affection. They learn to defer; they learn *not* to excel in male terms. They learn to curb their anger.[2]

This description of women's compliance with society's expectation fits Hearth Tender perfectly and Superwoman to a lesser extent.

Add the women's movement to the picture, and Superwoman is born.

Since its inception in the 1960s, the women's movement has raised the consciousness level and aspirations of American women. It became socially acceptable to look for opportunities beyond the home. Dreams could now become reality, and women were encouraged to match their skills with challenges from new fields. They were free to experiment with all of these prerogatives, which had been up to that time, exclusive male territory.

New magazines addressed themselves to the professional liberated woman and her needs. Established magazines realized that the new attitude and movement represented a potentially lucrative market. So under the sophisticated guise of self-help and the endless discussions of such topics as the problems working women encounter in juggling family and job and sex discrimination, these journals captured the attention of millions of women. By creating and marketing a very positive image of the modern woman who is upwardly mobile, popular magazines made most women feel glamorous and exciting.

In advertisements as well as in feature articles, women have been depicted as a new breed--reaching out for new adventures, new horizons, new levels of accomplishments, new pleasures—all uncompromisingly.

Lucy Komisar wrote in her article "The Image of Women in Advertising," in *Women in Sexist Society*, that advertising did not create these new images about women, but served as powerful reinforcement. It legitimized the many roles of the woman but also created false images of women that reflected male fantasies rather than reality. Komisar wrote, "The idealization of women is not much better than their derogation: goddesses are easily pulled off their pedestals and turned into temptresses and whores."[3]

Advertising, according to Komisar, acts on how people consciously perceive their roles so that it can get its message across. The strong message has been to emphasize the woman's role and to instill guilt in women who feel that their own lives and talents are more important than those of their families and husbands. The only way women can be "accepted" is to be all things to all people and to remember that relationships are more important than individual accomplishments, and that men are still dominant.

If the reader's eyebrows begin to rise in response to the previous paragraph's indictment of the advertising industry's pernicious influence, here is the astounding conclusion of a survey of the average housewife done by Haug Associates, Los Angeles, and printed in *Ad Age*:[4]

> She likes to watch television and she does not enjoy reading a great deal. She is most easily reached through television and the simple, down-to-earth magazines. She finds satisfaction within a rather small world and the center of this world is her home.
>
> She has little interest or skill to explore, to probe into things for herself. Her energy is largely consumed in the day-to-day living. She is very much open to suggestion and amenable to guidance that is presented in terms that fit in with her needs and with her view of the world.
>
> She tends to have a negative or anti-conceptual way of thinking. Mental activity is arduous for her. Her ability for inference particularly in unfamiliar areas is limited. And she tends to experience discomfort and confusion when faced with ambiguity or too many alternatives.
>
> She is a person who wants to have things she can believe in with certainty, rather than things she has to think about.

That average housewife-moron described above was targeted by advertising which exploited her insecurities and guilt.

And although the consuming public laughed about idiotic portrayals in specific ads, the unrelenting message underscored a set of values which women should have, a set of behaviors women should engage in, and society's image of women.

Hearth Tender bought into the system and continues to comply with that image and set of values and behavior.

With the women's movement, the advertising industry sensed a broadening market for women who chose to have careers. Advertisements began to depict women who were executives during the day and either devoted mothers at home or sex symbols at night. Ads show women as skydivers, stockbrokers, elegant socialites, as well as mothers with their children on camping trips.

Take, for example, *Elle* magazine's letter to potential subscribers:

Dear Reader:

You're waiting at the corner for the light to turn green.

On your right is a woman who'd love to look like you. To possess your vitality. To have your skin, your hair, your eyes.

On your left is a school girl who yearns to own everything you have on. The gold. The cashmere. The leather, the fragrance..

...and looking at you is a really great looking guy whose admiration for you is .. well, nearly x-rated.

In short, you're the envy of everyone. A woman who has it all. Youth. Style. Beauty. Charm. Intelligence. Sophistication. Ability. Enough money to buy most of the things you want. A rich and fulfilling life ahead that's just waiting to be lived to the fullest.

Elle helps you get the look. You know what works well for you. What doesn't.

Elle helps you get the feel. You discover beauty techniques for presenting yourself at your best. What to play up. What to play down. What the tricks are. You nourish your personality by giving yourself more to talk about—new books, new films, new places, new passions, new people.

Elle helps you get it all. The introduction. The interview. The audition. The job. The raise. The promotion. The invitation. The date. The proposal. The table smack next to the door where all the others come in and stop to carry on about how fabulous you're looking.

What woman could resist the tantalizing new image America says she should have? Everywhere she turns, she is being told that the new woman is active, alive, exciting in all aspects of her life. Even mothers making peanut butter sandwiches for their children in the backyard are represented as all-American cheerleaders. Anyone in real life who doesn't display that happy attitude at all times obviously is a grouch and a social outcast. Is it any wonder, then, that the American woman has adopted all the roles and attitudes represented through the media?

The average woman is quite intelligent. She knows that these advertisements are the ideal or the fantasy of some advertising executive. Cognitively, she really knows that, but emotionally, she wants to make that fantasy come true. So Superwoman was created by being nudged into the new mold without too much resistance. She felt that the world at large had embraced the concepts of the new woman and provided psychological reinforcement for her.

Superwoman is an appropriate term for Stage II because this woman is a product of the changing times. She represents the quintessential modern woman. This category includes women who have decided that they need more in their lives than the emotional and spiritual vacuum they perceive in Hearth Tenders. They have elected to seek definition of themselves through their own imperatives rather than those imposed by society. They have made conscious decisions to seek greater self-actualization.

Superwomen have acquired the skills to further their interests and careers. They are educated, trained, and employed in professions which require technical proficiency and high levels of analytical ability. By being in the job market Superwomen are aware of the women's movement and some of the problems women encounter both at home and at work. They have first-hand experience in juggling the demands of dual roles. In addition, unending self-help articles and books offer advice on meeting these demands by altering work schedules, priorities, and attitudes.

The Superwoman constantly seeks reasonable compromises to fill her many roles. And although Superwoman feels stressed out by her hectic pace, she feels reassured through the literature that she is not alone. She is part of the new legion of women who are exercising their options to be more fulfilled, and in doing so, she feels that she is enriching the lives of those around her. She feels that she represents a new breed of dynamic woman. The traditional lifestyle and value system do not meet her psychological and intellectual needs.

Because of her upbeat, can-do attitude, Superwoman feels that she has the energy and the strength to take on the world. She has acquired the enviable mindset that she wants to try everything and can do it all. As a result, she fills her day with a myriad of professional, civic, and family activities. Superwoman's most dominant characteristic, then, is her commitment to doing everything and being all things to all people.

Another element which distinguishes Superwoman is her willingness to succeed. She is fairly comfortable with her abilities and skills and knows that she is very competent. But she wants professional success on her own terms. She has subconsciously set her own boundaries and does not want to exceed those self-imposed limits. She has what has become popularly known as fear of success.

Fear of success (FOS) will be discussed later, but for now, it can be summarized as Superwoman's anxieties about the effects of success on her relationships with her friends and family.

With a life that is filled to the brim, Superwoman feels that her zest for living and her enthusiasm can compensate for any stressors or areas of dissatisfaction in her life. She does not seek outside training or help to expand her ability to deal with her broadened horizons. So, when she is exhausted or "feeling down," she either sublimates her sadness and fears or becomes depressed. Those strange feelings that "something is missing" or "I have a funny, empty feeling in my stomach," are noticed but not addressed.

Despite her progressive attitudes about her life and herself, Superwoman still uses the traditional coping mechanisms which Hearth Tender uses. What happens is that Superwoman—like Hearth Tender—keeps pent-up emotions which she feels the world at large does not appreciate in a woman. She feels guilty about being angry or depressed so she keeps those emotions repressed.

To summarize, Superwoman is a product of socialization and the new image projected through literature and advertising. Compared with Hearth Tender, Superwoman has come a long way and is more fully actualized and challenged. She has the ambition and training to succeed but she still operates within the limits she has set in her own mind. She is dynamic up to a point; she is successful up to a point; she is able to cope with the demands of life up to a point.

Superwoman is the starting point for the new modern woman. Her major characteristics are:

1. Doing it all—all things to all people
2. Fear of success
3. Traditional coping

Doing it all. Superwomen have the feeling that the world is open to them. Society has approved success for women through the women's movement, and media and advertising have reinforced this legitimacy through the widespread coverage and image they project. Superwomen are upbeat and optimistic about their prospects to succeed and feel that the fundamental cultural change in values works to their individual and collective advantage. All they have to do is to reach for that bright tomorrow.

Carol, 32, has moved up steadily in the competitive world of television reporting and has been a news anchor for over three years. The community viewers like her, and her presence on the news has increased the station's number of viewers.

Carol speaks with the confidence of a public personality, has the appearance and carriage which separate her from the average woman, dresses and talks like the dynamic and intelligent woman who she is.

"When I went to college, I knew that I wanted to be on the cutting edge of a growing industry. I majored in communications because I wanted to go into media work. I had figured out that television stations are keenly aware of their need to have women in prominent positions. They have an image to project; they can't have just middle-aged men as top newscasters in this day and age.

"I admit that I focused on television reporting since the time was right to have young women on the air in anchor spots.

"I interned at a television station one summer during college and studied the mannerisms, body language, speech styles, and dress of news anchors and program hosts. The people at the station were very kind and took me under their wing. They taught me tricks and let me tag along on assignments so that I could get a feel for putting stories together.

"After college, I applied for a television reporter job. I had an advantage over the other candidates since I was already familiar with the process and comfortable in front of the cameras. I got that job, and ten years later, here I am as a relatively successful news anchor."

Carol grew up during the initial excitement of the women's movement and developed goals and ambitions which reflected the attitude of the time. These were quite different from those of her parents.

Carol grew up in Indiana. Her father worked in a manufacturing plant, and her mother had a part-time job as a bakery assistant. Carol and her sister were brought up in the staunch Midwest conservative tradition. Roles for men and women were clearly understood, and nobody crossed the line.

"I remember my mother telling me that girls are not expected to be smart, just pretty and nice. It was the man's job to be clever and ambitious. Boy, that used to get me infuriated.

"If the women's movement and Betty Friedan hadn't come along, I would still be in Indiana, in the same town, married to one of the hometown boys, and the mother of a brood of kids."

Over her parent's objections Carol pursued excellence by distinguishing herself in academic, extracurricular, and sports activities in high school. She won a scholarship to college for her efforts.

"My dad always put me down for being on the top. He used to say, 'You are going to end up an old maid. No man wants to marry a genius. Why don't you just be like your mother. She takes care of me and you girls. That is the way it should be. Why do you have to be such a weirdo?'

"It really hurt my feelings that my own family didn't support what I was doing, but I couldn't picture myself following in my mother's footsteps. I would succeed, and then they would be proud of me."

Today Carol is a bright, articulate, and attractive woman. She is doing a terrific job in her profession and has an almost unlimited potential. She is aware of the special problems of women in a high-pressured, performance-oriented world. She is exceptionally proficient and is often more conscientious than her male counterparts. She has the world in the palm of her hand, but her self-designated Superwoman role will ultimately restrict both her professional and private lives.

Carol's problem is that she wants to do everything and wants to be all things to everyone. She stretches herself to the limit. Carol often serves as master of ceremony at local charitable fundraisers or as co-chairman of civic events. She tries to serve as a mentor and friend of the younger women reporters. She has dated Jim for the last five years and juggles her schedule to spend time with him. She works out at the health club a couple of times a week. Every minute of her time is fully scheduled.

Psychologist Phyllis Braiker points out in her book *The Type E Woman*, that women like Carol are heading toward a very self-destructive stress cycle. They push themselves relentlessly to do more, stretching their resources thinner and thinner. They simply can't say, "No."[5]

1. *All things to all people.* Superwomen have what Braiker called "excellence anxiety." Woman like Carol need to achieve success, but their success is almost always rated in terms of society's approval and acceptance rather than in their own terms. They need to please others and have status in the eyes of others. That is why Carol finds such satisfaction as a media personality. She finds more than just professional satisfaction; she finds ego gratification and identification from her position.

Carol's background has more of an influence that she knows. Subconsciously her parents and their values have had a lifelong effect on her, and although she has made a conscious effort to achieve and escape the gritty world of her childhood, the traditions are a permanent part of her value system and behavior.

Despite her air of control, Carol cannot say, "no." She is not comfortable in taking risks when it comes to her affiliation with people. She makes the extra effort to be easy to get along with.

Recently Jim and Carol had arranged to meet at their favorite restaurant for dinner after Carol finished the early evening television news. They have been dating each other for about five years and often meet for dinner during the week because Carol needs to get back to the studio for the late evening news.

Carol arrived at the restaurant, got a table, and ordered a glass of wine. She looked over the menu and said hello to the people who recognized her. She anticipated sharing the experiences of her day with Jim.

After Carol had been waiting for Jim for an hour, she got worried and started to imagine that something dreadful had happened to him. Fifteen minutes later, Jim bounded into the restaurant and sat down next to Carol.

"He acted as if nothing were the matter. He never even apologized for being over an hour late. He just launched into his usual questions about my day.

"I was annoyed that Jim was late and didn't even offer an explanation, but I didn't want to make an issue out of it. I figured that he had just had a very busy day and couldn't break away long enough to call me about being late."

Asked why she didn't express her anger to Jim, she responded, "I know that he must have had a very good reason. Besides, he would think that I was a bitch if I questioned him."

It turns out that Jim is often late or forgets that he has a date with Carol, but Carol remains understanding and never mentions her disappointment to Jim.

Carol is a typical Superwoman. She is nonassertive. She is unable to express her feelings honestly and allows people like Jim to take advantage of her. Anger is especially hard for her to deal with, because nonassertive women do not believe that anger is either a natural human emotion or feminine. When a Superwoman feels angry, she tries to deny this feeling and to suppress it. She doesn't express her anger because she has irrational ideas about anger. She really thinks that people will not like her as much, that they will retaliate with greater anger, or her image of being a sweet and nice person will be destroyed. Her self-esteem is tied to the view others have of her, so she denies or resists put-downs by others. She tries to be understanding of their points of view and criticisms of her. She rationalizes her behavior and shortcomings into virtues.

In her psychology practice, Harriet Braiker found that women categorically don't express anger or aggression as overtly as men. The Judith Bardwick study cited at the beginning of the chapter showed that young girls were less aggressive than boys and developed dependent tendencies, while boys were becoming more independent.

In many cases, women may not even recognize their feelings of anger. Instead, they disguise the rage or rationalize it like Carol. Psychiatrist Karen Horney called this behavior among women a neurotic need for affections and approval.[6] The wishes of others are more important than her own. She cannot assert herself in any way.

Assertiveness will be discussed in detail in another chapter, but its definition here will provide the reader with a short description. Assertiveness is the acquired ability to acknowledge your feelings—anger, sadness, hate, love, fear—and to deal with them honestly and openly with yourself. It is also the ability to respect yourself and others and their rights. It is an open and spontaneous recognition of your thoughts and feelings. These thoughts need not be conveyed to other people, but you must deal with them yourself. To sublimate or deny these thoughts or feelings would ultimately result in neurosis or depression or both.

Carol's great need for affiliation surfaced in a recent offer from the television station to promote her to news manager. She turned it down.

"I want to remain an 'on air' personality, and truthfully, I'm not sure that I could properly decide which stories would make the best news items. And, I don't like the idea of bossing my colleagues around."

This promotion caused Carol a great deal of stress. She had to evaluate herself, her achievements, her relationship to others. Further achievement became a threat to Carol. She was displaying fear of success. Her upbringing and her mother's haunting words that "it's a man's job to be clever and ambitious. Girls just have to be pretty and nice," played an important role in her turning down the promotion. She had been taught that women shouldn't be too ambitious and competitive. Women should be feminine and passive.

Carol described her mental struggle about assuming such a big leadership role: "I had a nagging feeling that 'I shouldn't be doing this. This is too tough. I will lose all of my old friends. Nobody will like me if I am the boss,' so I turned the job down."

It's hard to believe that a woman as young and bright as Carol would be a nonassertive person, but her behavior and attitude are unmistakable. By looking to others for verification of her identity,

Carol restricts her own life. She has to compromise her real needs, feelings, and ambitions and cannot strike out on her own and enjoy doing anything by herself. She is actually very dependent and psychologically helpless.

As Karen Horney stated in her book *Self Analysis*, women often limit their lives within narrow boundaries and are willing to take second or third place. These women—Superwomen—cannot assert themselves in any way. Pleasing others and retaining their goodwill takes precedence over their own goals and needs. Horney concludes that the general suppression of Superwoman's feelings and wishes results in her living beneath her means in every way—socially, economically, professionally, and emotionally. Psychologically, the results are equally unsatisfactory. She lowers her self-confidence and maintains a subconscious discontentment with herself and life.[7]

People like Jim sense this vulnerability in Carol. Although he gives lip service to his pride in dating an independent, smart woman and is generous on the surface, he actually tramples on her dignity because he knows he can get away with it.

While friendships and networks give women a chance to progress and to take risks, they keep the Superwoman in a subservient, stagnant postion. She has neither the confidence in her abilities nor the independence to risk new challenges.

Beyond the veneer Carol has very little self-confidence. She really believes that she needs to be friendly and nice all of the time, has no rights, and should never express anger or hostility.

2. *Compulsive dependence.* Amy, on the other hand, suffers from what Horney calls compulsive dependence.[8] Her entire world revolves around someone, usually a male. She expects this male to supply content to her life and take responsibility for her. She has the Cinderella syndrome.

Amy, 34, has elected to give up a promising career as dress designer to devote most of her energy and time to her new husband. Amy had pursued a career as a dress designer right after college. She volunteered to work on weekends, to be part of the sales team, to do all the unpleasant assignments nobody else wanted. By the time she was 28, she headed a major department of sportswear design. At that time, she met and became involved with a man who so enchanted her that she moved to his hometown and put her career on the back burner.

After a few years the relationship dissolved traumatically—he would not leave his wife to marry Amy. Amy was left with concentrating all of her energies on her career. Very quickly she met and married someone else and quit her job altogether. Now all she wants to do is to "devote quality time to my marriage."

Amy is bright and savvy on the surface. But she conceded that she "played the role of the helpless little girl and deliberately was manipulative and deceptive with the company bigwigs so that I would be promoted. I felt that I had the talent but the little feminine extras would help my career along. In the end, I got burned out, and I am not so sure that I will ever go back full-time. The only compensation was that the little girl act really works and I was rewarded for my performance."

Amy grew up in South Carolina and was the only daughter of the town's Cadillac dealer. He doted on his "little sweet pea."

"Daddy gave me anything I wanted; he always came to my rescue. I was his favorite child because my brother was always getting into trouble. And when my brother tried to take it out on me, Daddy told him that girls and women need to be treated with kindness and respect. And if he didn't remember that, Daddy would take away his privileges. Needless to say, I grew up thinking that women were a very special and delicate breed. We could do no wrong. What worked with Daddy would work with every other man. Boy, did life teach me a hard lesson to the contrary!"

When Amy entered the working world, she, like Carol, was determined to succeed. She would put in as many hours as necessary to impress her boss that she was capable and had a go-getter attitude. But after six years of this round-the-clock schedule at work, she was actually exhausted and suffering from chronic stress without realizing it. So, when Prince Charming came along, it was a perfect time to ease off. After all, she had already shown her worth and abilities in the industry, and if she wanted to remain and rise to the top, she felt that it was hers for the asking. But now was the time to settle down with a man she adored.

Both Braiker and Horney agree that Superwomen like Amy exposed themselves to unremitting stress over long periods. The end result is depression, anxiety, and burnout. Horney goes on to state that women like Amy have a neurotic need for partners who will take care of them the way daddy did.[9] It is a reversion to her upbringing and the values which were instilled during childhood. Those early years molded Amy to expect men to take care of and protect her. As long as she lived up to her father's expectations of women, she could thrive. By experience and intuition Amy learned to cope with the environment and learned to manipulate others effectively. Amy is a perfect example of the socialization Bardwick researched.

Amy now expects her new husband to fill the voids in her life, to take responsibility for her well-being and happiness, and to solve all of her problems.

According to Horney this compulsive dependency is based primarily on Superwoman's expectations. She wants to be taken care of so that she won't have to make decisions; she won't have to hustle or take the initiative. She doesn't want to be responsible for herself. The Amys of the world decide to become helpless so that someone—usually a man—will rescue them.

The broad tradition of society designated the roles for men and women as both Carol's and Amy's fathers did. It is therefore not surprising that both women look to men for verification and protection. They were raised to think that men are more important and powerful than women. It is reassuring for them to feel that the world accepts and approves of the roles of the protective masculine figure and the helpless female figure.

The role of men and their attitudes are important pieces of the whole as they relate to the psychological state of women. The women's movement and advertising are only two components influencing today's woman. Men and their attitudes toward women are also significant factors.

Regardless of their psychological stage of development, most women have been exposed to and influenced by the attitudes of each parent's role in the home, the interrelationship between parents, and what was considered appropriate behavior for girls and women in the family. That unspoken value system and demonstrated behavior served as powerful examples of "the way it should be."

We know that the Hearth Tender used her family's values and activities as models for her own adult life. Superwoman, although trying to break out of her traditional upbringing, has not made a complete transformation and remains quite conventional in some important areas.

Studies and research have shown that societies all over the world socialize men and women differently. Nancy Chodorow in her article "Being and Doing: A Cross-Cultural Examination of Socialization of Males and Females," asserts that research results show that there are no absolute personality differences between men and women. But the designated roles in society assign women the primary tasks of family and child care as the primary socializers. Through history men have established themselves institutionally and culturally as more prestigious and privileged than women and their activities.[10]

Karen Horney, who was probably the first feminist, wrote in 1932 that since the mother is the principal voice of approval or disapproval, boys had to reject their mothers at some point in their lives in order to gain independence. She called this "Dread of Women."[11] Horney adds that men subconsciously feel that women are more powerful, since they can bear children and for centuries managed the crucial tasks of existence such as raising the children, growing the food, weaving the cloth and sewing the clothes, and keeping the family together. In essence, Horney's theory is the feminist psychological counterpart of Freud's Penis Envy.

Ironically, Horney was a colleague of Freud prior to emigrating to the United States from Europe and as early as the 1920s began to refute some of Freud's theories about women and their problems.

Even if we were to dismiss Horney's theory about "Dread of Women," the fact remains that societies generally have designated superior roles for men and subordinate roles for women.

Today in America men are made aware of their gender superiority from boyhood on. Studies by both Sandra Bem[12] and Judith Bardwick[13] show fairly conclusively that boys begin gaining self-esteem and independence as early as the age of five, while girls remain dependent without a clear definition of their identity.

It is not surprising, then, that men and their attitudes toward women are extremely strong influences on the value systems and behavioral patterns of women. Of course, fathers are the primary influencers, but men who are professionally or financially successful also have a strong effect on women and the roles they assume.

Take Harold, for example. At 60 years old, he is a self-made man who has risen from a small-town boy to an urban industrialist. He serves as a chairman of the boards of many corporations and is regarded as both successful and powerful.

Debonair, sophisticated, and very courtly, Harold built his empire by approaching both social and business dealings the same way: with vigor and forcefulness. He has succeeded in over 95 percent of his business dealings, and his reputation in the business world is without reproach. At the same time, this industrial scion also influences others with his attitude toward women.

A handsome man with an eye for women, Harold has never had any difficulty attracting women, but as a product of the time when sex roles were more clearly defined than they are now, he is often perplexed about the women's movement:

Women should be able to do whatever they want, and it would be hypocritical to assume that men can do whatever they want and that a different set of rules applies to women. They have needs and wants too. But I think that the solution to this entire liberation movement is for women to have sex three times a week. If more women were sexually satisfied, they wouldn't be running around trying to find satisfaction in other areas. I think that many women will never be sexually satisfied because they are uptight and psychologically frigid.

For a man who grew up in a very prescribed social environment in which women served the needs of their families, Harold's last sentence captured some of the essence of the problem Superwomen have. Women who don't have a strong sense of identity and purpose are insecure and suffer from a poor self-image. Indeed they are "psychologically frigid" and constantly succumb to men like Harold. After all, Harold is a powerful leader and women believe in him unquestioningly.

Harold is an intelligent man and knows that society accepts self-actualization among women as part of the modern movement. He pays lip service to women seeking their own careers and destinies in the same breath that he expresses his opinion that women need sexual satisfaction more than careers. His mixed message confuses many women, and they fall easy prey to his power and success and his line that "I find it exciting to seduce an attractive, intelligent, and feminine woman."

Alice Wilson Schaef wrote in *Women's Reality* that these women carry the lifelong burden of feeling powerless and inferior because they grew up in what they perceived to be a male-dominated society. These women need male validation and approval of their activities. They believe that connection to and acceptance by a male will insure their survival.[14]

Bolstered by the attitudes and actions of men like Harold, Superwomen continue to rely inordinately on men to provide them with an identity.

Even younger men like Carol's friend Jim and industrialist Fred, 45, ultimately find it irresistable to seduce Superwomen psychologically and physically.

Fred is a modern success story, a living example of a Horatio Alger hero. From the time he was ten years old, Fred had decided that he would be a millionaire by the time he was 30. He worked alongside migrant workers as a bean picker in the summers, made birdhouses for sale at the local garden store, earned recognition as an Eagle Scout, and started a lawn maintenance business—all before he graduated from high school. He went to college in Ohio on a track scholarship and developed his "wheeler-dealer" skills while there. After college he took a job as a salesman for a national company. Two years later, he started his first company. By the time he was 34, he and his partner had become one of the largest, privately held corporations in the country.

A charming man with a flair for the dramatic, Fred is sought out by everyone. He serves on charity boards, college boards of trustees, chairs major industrial conferences, works with foundations to further their goals, as well as looks for new ways to expand his own corporation.

"As a guy who came from nowhere to success, I am a living example that all things are possible in America. Talent just is. It can and does come from all areas irrespective of sex, color, heritage.

"Women's identity has been defined by men up to this point, but women have very great talents. They are more sensitive to feelings because they can produce life. Men are too combative; women are great problem solvers.

"Men have reacted quite violently to the threat they perceive from competent, accomplished women. So men exclude women from their activities. Men consolidate their position. And truthfully, some militant feminists have turned men away from their potential support for women.

"You know the old saying, 'no pain, no gain.' Women realize that this is a temporary situation and in the end they will be able to achieve whatever they want. Younger men and women are increasingly aware of talent and accept each other's ambitions and goals with respect."

Fred conceded that his attitudes about professional women and opportunities for them are probably more broad-minded than most because he has always owned his business. He never had to compete for a position or try to outsell his strategy against a woman.

When it comes to the social setting, however, Fred reverts back to a very traditional set of values.

"I find it very difficult to resist an attractive woman in a social setting. And sometimes even in business I temper myself when dealing with a pretty woman. I start thinking about her as a woman rather than as a professional peer."

As a young magnetic multimillionaire, Fred takes full advantage of his attractiveness to women. He has been able to effortlessly indulge his insatiable appetite for women. And here again, as with Harold, women receive a mixed message from a successful man. He articulates his philosophy about talent and the equality of the sexes at the same time he flirts, flatters, and seduces as many women as he can.

Why do educated, professional women fall for these men? As we pointed out earlier, women continue to depend on others to verify their attractiveness and intelligence. And when successful men compliment them, they feel that they are more worthy than when less successful men pay attention to them.

As Judith Bardwick points out, boys develop a sense of self early and turn to the outer world for confirmation of their achievements and self-esteem. Girls' cultural values and characteristic responses destine them to remain dependent on others for definition and affirmation. Superwomen then perpetuate the powerful, mythical conception of American womanhood by believing that their lives and activities are not as important as those of men.[15]

Fear of Success. Superwomen have fear of success (FOS). Like Carol who gave up a promotion at the television station, Superwomen feel that if they are too successful they will lose their friends and become less feminine. In addition, their behavior systems, which include more passive roles, and their compulsive dependence would make success uncomfortable for them.

Fear of success is a term used to describe the psychological block women develop when they become high achievers. These women conjure up images of disastrous results if they assert themselves and are self-initiators. Just as in the classic study,[16] by Matina Horner, Superwomen feel that if they continue to excel in the professional world, they will become less feminine, less popular, have a terrible accident that will maim them for life, or some other catastrophe. These fears may be vague and unarticulated in some women, which makes them potentially even more vulnerable.

The connection between success and being unfeminine results in fear of success. The connection can be explained as follows: success requires achievement behavior, achievement behavior requires competitive behavior, competitive behavior is one form of aggressive behavior, and aggressive behavior is regarded by society as unfeminine behavior. Success is therefore also unfeminine behavior. This conflict creates avoidance behavior in situations that involve success both now or in the future.

Although Horner's pioneer work in the area of fear of success was an axiom of gender role differences for a long time, the many studies that have been done since the 1960s indicate that females in stages beyond Stage II do not show more fear of success imagery than males. But Superwomen definitely have a great fear of success.

Just what is fear of success, and why is it so devastating to human progress? Research tells us that FOS is an irrational reaction to doing well and moving ahead. A person with FOS truly believes that disasters will happen if she continues to be successful, and in order to survive, she must stop being successful.

FOS stems from the common superstition that the higher one goes, the farther one will fall. FOS occurs in both men and women and usually has its origins in a person's upbringing and becomes a very strong part of the person as an adult.

There are basically three major themes that might indicate the presence of FOS. The first category is fear of social rejection. For women like Carol, it is fear of losing friends if she accepts the promotion. She actually feels that she will be less desirable as a woman and will become lonely and isolated. To avoid such a prospect Carol chooses to camouflage her strengths and talents.

The second category focuses on a woman's doubts about being normal and her guilt about success. The traditional values are so ingrained in Superwoman that she feels that her professional success exceeds the boundaries of the system in which she grew up. The role of the traditional woman is clearly defined to center around serving others, not oneself. So when a woman is successful, she experiences great stress and guilt. She, in fact, does not want to stand out from the crowd; she does not want to arouse suspicion and envy among her friends; rather, she wants to be accepted as a conventional woman, one of the gang.

Women university students who are Superwomen feel guilty when they excel. They feel guilty that they are doing better than their male classmates. Goldberg found that college women valued the professional work of men more highly than the identical work of women when the professions were law, city planning, and medicine.

The first study done by Matina Horner in 1964 produced results which definitely indicated how traditional women view success.

The women students in her course in introductory psychology were asked to write creative stories to the following scenario: "At the end of the first term finals, Anne finds herself at the top of her medical school class."

Student replies included examples of both denial of effort and responsibility and bizarre outcomes for Anne.

Anne is really happy she's on top, though Tom is higher than she. That's as it should be. Anne doesn't mind Tom winning.

It is luck that Anne came out on top of her med class because she didn't want to go to medical school anyway.

She starts proclaiming her surprise and joy. Her fellow classmates are so disgusted with her behavior that they jump on her body and beat her. She is maimed for life.

These student reactions to Anne's success reflect the strong psychological and emotional resistance to successful women.

When there is success, women summon up a very sophisticated system of denial of effort and responsibility for success. This is the third category of FOS.

Superwomen use the self-deprecation and self-criticism to temper their success. "I am only a housewife." "I was just lucky." "Anybody could have done that." They refuse to take proper credit for their accomplishments and their skills.

Sally had gone to medical school as a young 20-year-old Phi Beta Kappan. She spent the first three years of medical school accumulating the top grades in her class. It had always been her dream to become a cardiovascular surgeon. Not many women are surgeons, and fewer still are in the field of heart surgery.

After graduating at the top of her class, Sally had an outstanding internship year. When it came time for a residency in surgery, Sally suddenly became very argumentative with the surgical staff, questioned procedures, and performed poorly in general surgery.

Sally ultimately became a pediatrician. She felt that it was a more acceptable field for women physicians.

"I didn't want the stress and discomfort of having to excel constantly," Sally explained. "I wasn't prepared to meet my own standards. Besides, I don't want to be an outcast among women physicians by specializing in a man's field—surgery. I know that I will like pediatrics."

Jane, too, was a brilliant student. She received honors in all of her courses. When she was scheduled to take her Ph.D. written exams, everyone expected her to come through with flying colors. Instead, she panicked. "I couldn't think. I went into a trance. I just got up and left the exams. I guess I didn't want a doctorate after all."

FOS occurs among Superwomen because they want to remain dependent and don't want to be responsible for their own lives. They retreat to a fall back position because it is less taxing professionally and safer socially.

Although Horner's theory has intuitive appeal and has been accepted as though it were proven, subsequent research asserts that FOS is not deep-seated in women's personality. Rather, FOS is situationally determined.

In her article, "Psychometric Properties and Underlying Assumptions of Four Objective Measures of FOS," Michelle Paludi concludes that the occupation in which success is achieved needs to be consistent with sex role appropriateness. Negative imagery is projected onto women who succeed in non-traditional female settings such as medicine. However, if subjects are allowed to define success for themselves, they exhibit relatively little FOS and there is *no* significant difference in the amount of FOS projected by men and women.

Paludi and Tresemer state that the phrase *fear of success* attracts attention, but research has shown that:

1. FOS and sex role orientation appear to be unrelated.
2. No reliable age or sex differences in FOS have been observed.
3. It is not clear whether FOS is a motive or cultural stereotype.
4. FOS has shown no relationship to ability in women.
5. There is no consistent relationship between FOS and any behavioral measure.[17]

While psychological research has shown that FOS is inconclusive, it does, however, apply to Superwomen because they are so steeped in sex role stereotypes that occupational and academic deviations from those roles cause them great discomfort.

Take the case of Sue, a young advertising account executive. She had been quite successful in promoting the products of her clients, and their sales had increased substantially as a result of her efforts. The top management at the ad agency noticed her talent in marketing, and soon she was handling larger and larger accounts.

Her first recognition of her progress in the company was a new office. She was to be given a large office with a window and posh furniture. Her colleagues told Sue that the quality of her work was what counted, not the physical space in which she worked. After all, she wouldn't want to separate herself from her buddies by moving to a big executive office, would she? And she wouldn't like to demoralize the older account executives by having an office which was better than theirs, would she?

Sue agreed and continued to occupy the small cubicle she had had since she started with the company.

Sue's co-workers were able to keep her in her place by intimating that an office of power would result in losing her friends. She would be held responsible for the morale of the office staff, if she moved to fancier surroundings.

As soon as she capitulated on the issue of her office, the rest of the office knew just how to keep her in her place. Top management felt that Sue didn't want to move ahead, since she turned down one of the perks of a rising star, so Sue became stalemated. Her progress stopped.

By not standing up for an executive office, Sue thought she was demonstrating that she was easy to get along with and was a member of the team. She did not realize that subconsciously she valued cameraderie more than upward mobility in the company.

It is clear that Superwomen are not propelled by a great need for professional success. There is also strong evidence that they are interested in neither power nor money.

Of 450 women public school administrators who were surveyed in North Carolina, few showed interest in power and money and were primarily interested in helping others and making a difference.

Sara, 35, an elementary school supervisor, summed it up:

> I have a strong desire to do a good job at whatever I am doing and to be helpful to others. As a result, I am willing to work hard and work with others to get the job done. Getting the job done and helping others is my primary interest, rather than inflating ego and wanting power.

Harriet, 51, a general supervisor in the school system, never felt the need for promotions or higher salaries:

> I try to do my best on any assignment and follow through to the end. I have pride in what I do and am persistent in getting all the facts. I am a low-key person, easy to work with, and make it a point to maintain harmony in working relationships.
>
> I do not seek to be the leader but am a good support person who can do a lot of leg work and get information to help someone else fulfill a task.
>
> I am professional, dependable, and most people find it easy to trust me.

Both Harriet and Sarah articulate clearly and honestly what they believe to be their strengths and values. And they speak for millions of women who were raised within the framework of traditional female values.

These values have historically been consistent with earth survival. These are not simply female values, but are values that have always been vitally needed to survive as human beings. Many centuries later the Superwoman is still a "civilizer"; she undertakes innumerable roles and seeks to serve and please others. For her efforts, Superwoman stunts her own growth, development, and happiness.

Traditional coping. Superwoman approaches her life within the construct of her traditional upbringing, and in doing so she develops that "empty feeling" and realizes that "something is missing" in her life.

While the Hearth Tender was brought up in the same environment, she is relatively satisfied with her life because she is not trying to be everything to everybody. Rather, the boundaries of her life were established for her early in life, and she is content to live within that emotional and psychological area. Her life is much simpler than that of the Superwoman, because Hearth Tender is not tantalized or agonized by the images of the new woman or the pressure to compete in the professional world. She lives her life relatively oblivious to the problems Superwoman encounters.

On the other hand, Superwoman charted an ambitious life course for herself and has been reasonably successful. She has the education and experience to do an excellent job professionally. She has sought self-actualization to make her life fuller. She is trying to fulfill that image in her mind that she can have it all.

Superwoman's major stumbling block is that she has not acquired the coping skills to deal with the stressors she has imposed on herself. She has bought into just part of the new woman—the professional and multi-role part—and has failed to learn how to deal with the emotionally and psychologically hard situations.

Television anchorwoman Carol feels uneasy despite the praise and respect she has gained from her job.

"I don't know what is wrong with me. The public seems to like me. The ratings are up for our program. I do a lot of public appearances as a celebrity, and I always enjoy meeting people. But it seems that the more I do, the less satisfied I feel. On the job and in my own life, I try to be an upbeat, cheerful, and active person.

"I must be doing something wrong because I am not totally satisfied with my life. I am physically fit, but I am exhausted. Maybe it's my spirit. Maybe I need to regroup and figure this all out."

Carol is not alone when she expresses her inability to identify what is bothering her. Superwomen by their nature were raised without the tools to deal with anxiety and conflict. Even though they represent a new generation of women who are forging new professional and personal frontiers, Superwomen need to know that they grew up in traditional families—families in which women believed that they should neither get angry nor express anger when they feel it. The tradition included suppression of hostility, a subconscious ideal of the way women "should" behave, and a constant feeling that they are responsible for the well-being of everyone they know.

Superwomen can be described as feminist lemmings. They have been overly influenced by exaggerations made by extremists, so they were caught up by the vocabulary, the energy, and the drama of the women's movement. But they have not grasped the nature of the real change. That is why they are often confused, anxious, and at odds with themselves. As psychiatrist Helen DeRosis summed it up, "These women, in their pursuit of what they consider their rightful liberties, have lost touch with civility and common sense."[18]

The Superwoman represents an overreaction to the women's movement because she reaches for all the glamor and glitz but doesn't have the interpersonal training or psychological frame of mind to cope adequately with the multiple roles she has assumed. Like lemmings, Superwomen rush pell mell over the cliff following the pressure of being everything they can be—without knowing what lies ahead.

DeRosis contends that the woman who has severe emotional conflicts is constantly divided and exhausted by them. She tries to relieve these conflicts by denying them and not dealing with them directly.[19] Instead, she creates an imaginary self who is admirable, virtuous, and perfect. These perfectionistic standards control her life. She does more and more and achieves less and less satisfaction—like Carol.

Both Phyllis Chesler and Helen DeRosis have done a great deal of clinical work with depressed women. Many of them are Superwomen. These women are like Carol and Amy, who absorb abuse from others without expressing their own feelings. They end up internalizing these very intense emotions of anger and sadness; they don't express their disappointment; they continue to feel responsible for the well-being of others and deny their own needs. The result is depression. Because of their irrational fears that nobody will like them if they get angry, most of the Superwomen walk around with an enormous emotional overload that never subsides. If and when they do explode, they suffer from such guilt that they become overly submissive as though they were doing penance for their outbursts.

Psychiatrists like DeRosis and Horney and psychologists who work with depressed women all agree that most of these Superwomen have brought this depression on themselves because they are not honest with themselves about their feelings and deny that anything is wrong. These women are nonassertive and assume passive and semihelpless roles.

Many Superwomen live their lives through others—co-workers, husbands, children, civic groups. Their identity rests with others. Others' accomplishments become Superwoman's accomplishments derivatively, and their failures make her feel worthless and depressed. Since she takes personal responsibility for their needs, she believes that their failings must reflect her incompetence.

To avoid failure and the criticism that goes with it, Superwoman works at everything and fills as many roles as she can. By working to please everyone, she hopes to avoid criticism. Superwoman actually believes that she has no rights of any kind and therefore tries to be passive, compliant, and nice at all times. She allows others to take advantage of her and to violate her rights. This totally nonassertive behavior results in hostility, depression, and guilt about not fulfilling the role which she believes society has designated for her.

In Chesler's article "Patient and Patriarch: Women in the Psychotherapeutic Relationship," she notes that clinical case histories show that women are chronically fatigued and/or depressed. They suffer from headaches and feelings of inadequacy. If left untreated, mild depression will get worse and result in hysteria, paranoia, and frigidity. These women express a harsh, self-critical, self-depriving, and often self-destructive set of attitudes.

Chesler feels that more women than men seek psychiatric help because society allows women to display emotional and physical distress more easily than men. She thinks that psychotherapy along with marriage are the only two socially approved institutions for middle-class women. Both marriage and therapy represent unequal relationships and isolate women from each other. Both are based on a woman's helplessness and dependence on a stronger male authority figure, and both control and oppress women. These are two safe havens for women in a society that seems to offer them no others.[20] Chesler's opinion appear to be extreme and may be only partially valid, but as in all reform movements—of which the women's movement is one—radical views are often needed in order to sensitize the public.

Superwomen do, in fact, suffer from depression and anxiety. They almost never know that they are depressed. And if they have a feeling that they might be depressed, they seldom admit their depression. The underpinning philosophy of our social system is so strong that women still perceive themselves to be the nurturers in all their roles.

To accomplish less creates confusion and frustration in these women.

Margaret Adams, like Phyllis Chesler, also feels that this "compassion trap" is designed to keep women in both practical and emotional bondage. In "The Compassion Trap," she states that society has sold women a line that they are the warm earth mothers and therefore have to subordinate their individual needs to the welfare of others.[21] Society actually has imposed a fear of success on Superwoman because it has conditioned her into thinking that her nurturing role is more important than her own ambitions.

Adams concludes that Superwoman's function in the compassion trap is "being plundered to prolong moribund life of a corrupt and decaying social order."[22] In fact, all the nurturing by women has not changed the world's basic destructive, exploitative nature.

Distilling the extremist views of Adams and Chesler, it is clear that Superwomen are women in transition. These new women have not yet found their places. Psychiatrists like DeRosis feel that they will not find their places until they decide where, what, and who they are at any given time. In trying to be a new woman in all respects, Superwomen are trying to actualize a new fantasy of perfection.

When Superwoman finally realizes that she cannot be all things to all people, she must come to grips with the facts that her real life does not fulfill her life fantasy. She will never live up to the perfectionist demands she has set for herself. She will then begin to experience great feelings of anxiety and hopelessness. DeRosis feels that this hopelessness in Superwomen results from their lost dreams. For the woman like Amy whose life revolves around her husband, for example, the lost dreams center around the fact that she cannot accept him for what he is. She reasons that if she is to become the wonderful and perfect woman of her dreams, than her husband should be wonderful and perfect too.

Amy persuaded her husband, Dan, to move his job and home to South Carolina after they were married. Dan, 55, had established a prosperous sales territory and had roots in Tennessee, but because he wanted to make the marriage successful, he consented.

For a while Amy and Dan lived with Amy's parents until they could find new jobs and a home. Interestingly, Dan started having severe chest pains, headaches, and developed dangerously high blood pressure. Amy explained, "I think Dan's body is trying to make the adjustment from the mountains to our lowland climate and humidity. Once he gets used to it, he will be fine."

Amy and Dan found a house and began renovating it. Dan was hired as a manufacturer's representative, and Amy was hired as a part-time sportswear designer, the field in which she had once been a rising star. But Dan started having trouble in his sales district, since he was new to the area. Other salesmen had long-standing personal relationships with clients, so Dan had difficulty penetrating the market. He finally quit his job because of his frustration and because his health still has not improved. "I guess Dan has become Mr. Wonderful with tarnished edges," says Amy of the latest developments. "Maybe my fairy-tale life and fairy-tale marriage are not going to come true."

Amy's parents, like many parents of Hearth Tenders, did a great disservice to her by treating her as a little princess. Although she is bright, talented, and charming, Amy reverts back to the childhood dreams and visions which her parents instilled in her as a young girl.

Modern sophisticates may scoff at the notion of fairy tales and lost dreams in an age of self-fulfillment, equal opportunities, and ever-new frontiers for women to explore. Yet the examples in this chapter and practices of clinical psychologists and psychiatrists can and do verify the existence of these fantasies through the thousands of depressed women they treat every year.

Superwomen are realistic enough to judge themselves by those accepted barometers of success that the rest of the world uses: power, money, prestige, success. Where they fall short is the level of success and goals they set for themselves. Since they were encouraged by the women's movement to "reach for the stars" and that all things are possible, superwoman sets her sights on horizons that can never be reached. She invests time, effort, talent, enthusiasm, and all her psychic resources into the process. But that still is not enough. She still comes up feeling empty and has an unidentifiable frustration with her life.

Through no fault of her own, Superwoman is a creation of both traditional and new values. She is neither fish nor fowl. She is no longer the Hearth Tender, because she wants the unlimited world that the women's movement and the media tell her is hers for the asking. But she is not yet a Boat Rocker because she hasn't come to grips with the psychological and emotional conflicts and stressors she encounters in her world. Her basic value system is still quite traditional, while her lifestyle is part of the modern woman. She finds herself precariously situated between two worlds, two value systems, two behavioral modes. The result is a life which has some professional and personal success--but also a great deal of professional and personal dissatisfaction.

Superwoman has come a long way from Hearth Tender, but still has an even longer way to go to be comfortable with herself.

Stage III:
Beyond Superwoman

The term Beyond Superwoman sounds like advertising hype used to describe an improved product—beyond superlative. It could easily bring to mind an image of a female caped crusader ever vigilant and ready to help all who ask. She can cook, clean, deliver brilliant research papers, perform neurosurgery with equal skill. She could be the model for the humorous caricatures of the "new woman" seen so often in advertisements on television and sometimes in prime-time series.

But the term here has a more modest meaning. Beyond Superwoman refers to Stage III of development and is the next stage of psychological progression past Hearth Tender and Superwoman. Beyond Superwomen are no longer confined by the traditional passive behavior of the Hearth Tender. And unlike Superwoman, Beyond Superwoman is no longer worried about pleasing everyone or losing friends if she advances in her profession.

This category includes those women who have a much firmer grasp of their abilities and professional prospects as well as confidence in their interpersonal skills. They have examined the simplistic fabric of traditional female behavior and opted for a world of expanded choices.

Beyond Superwoman has taken an objective look at reality and has identified the problems women have encountered in the paths of their career advancement. Unlike Hearth Tender and Superwoman, Beyond Superwoman knows that if it takes both hard work and political savvy to overcome those obstacles, charm and sincerity won't do it. This is the first stage in which we can identify women who have systematically evaluated the barriers to their careers and have decided to overcome them.

Fully aware of the opportunities and obstacles women face, Beyond Superwomen, through trial and error, have developed skills with which to handle their professional and personal problems. They have had very little formal training in assertiveness, time management, and stress management. Consequently, the coping mechanisms used by Beyond Superwomen vary from a soft, nonthreatening style to a strong no-nonsense approach. Each Beyond Superwoman's style is personal and idiosyncratic.

Most Beyond Superwomen are well educated professionals who have achieved some leadership and power, but do not necessarily want to go beyond that level. Primarily they want to get along in their own universe and attain a reasonable level of personal satisfaction and challenge in their professions. If the world changes for the better, that is fine, but Beyond Superwoman is not driven to bring about change by taking great personal risks. She does not want to be a crusader for issues or causes if it jeopardizes her present position of effectiveness. She does not actively seek out leadership roles.

Another characteristic of Beyond Superwoman is that she does not feel social or psychological pressures to assume the sex stereotyped role of Hearth Tender or the many roles of Superwoman. Beyond Superwoman is much more honest in her assessment of her limitations and her willingness to be pressured into conventional female roles. Where Hearth Tender and Superwoman fall easily into the roles society expects of them, Beyond Superwoman doesn't feel at all compelled to play the game. She feels more comfortable with herself as an individual than do Stage I and Stage II women and is therefore freer to determine her own behavior. She has relatively good control and power over her own life.

Beyond Superwoman is also distinguished from the previous stages in another way: although she started her career without clear goals, Beyond Superwoman has been quite successful. She is relatively satisfied and comfortable with her accomplishments. She accepts all the responsibilities and hard work that got her where she is. She does not dismiss her achievements as "just lucky," as Superwoman does.

Beyond Superwoman also accepts the level of power she has achieved in her job. She neither apologizes nor feels guilty about the power she has attained through her expertise and position.

In summarizing the characteristics that distinguish Beyond Superwoman from Hearth Tender and Superwoman, Beyond Superwoman has: (1) Become aware of problems women face. (2) Developed her own modus operandi and personal style. (3) No fear of success and has risen to leadership and power. Beyond Superwoman is totally comfortable with her accomplishments. She determines her own personal destiny and takes responsibility for her own actions.

Awareness of problems

Beyond Superwomen have no illusions about smooth sailing in either the professional or personal areas. They do not convince themselves that they will receive proper recognition and promotion for their efforts as Superwomen do. They feel that degrading themselves into a sex stereotyped role will, in the long run, be detrimental to both their careers and their psychological well-being.

For their own survival, most Beyond Superwomen have identified with unusual clarity and objectivity the major obstacles that block their personal and career development.

1. Career obstacles resulting from family demands. A large number of Beyond Superwomen listed this as a key factor which made life more strenuous and stressful.

> Dealing with a husband who is not supportive of my career is probably my biggest problem. It creates tensions and pressures for me and detracts from my best efforts on the job. If I have to stay late for a meeting, I know that I'll get angry comments when I get home.
> He'll say things like, "I've been waiting for dinner for hours or don't you care what happens to me? Maybe the office is more important than I am."
> My husband is very good at inflicting guilt. Even after thirty years, he still has problems recognizing that I am a professional who has difficult responsibilities. It has been very hard to mix a career and family.
> *Lisa, 57, project director*

> Both my husband and parents didn't approve of my career. My husband is slowly beginning to share some of the household duties, but my parents remain dead set against my working. They tell me that I should work only if I have to. They feel that I am degraded by having to be in the job market, instead of staying home and being the lady of the manor.
> *Ginny, 38, laboratory researcher*

> Home duties have been my most difficult obstacle. Making sure my children were taken care of properly while I was at work was my greatest worry. Spending time with the children

and my husband during the evenings and weekends meant that I had to eliminate my participation in a lot of meetings at work. I know this decision cost me quite a few promotions.
Catherine, 47, middle manager

2. *Supervisors who don't recognize the efforts of women and don't encourage them through coaching, career counseling, or feedback on performance.*

My background of experiences and educational level are superior to those of most of my cohorts. I always have bubbling energy while others project an indifferent or lazy attitude. But my supervisor never gives me challenging assignments and never gives me advice on how to get ahead. I know I am not utilized properly. This situation is encouraging me to leave my field.
Karen, 42, middle line manager

I have never been informed of important decisions that affect my responsibilities as a manager. My boss does not fulfill his job and blames me if reports are late. It's hard to meet a deadline if you are told that you'll be informed when the date is decided. And then no one tells you.
Hazel, 63, project director

3. *Organizational barriers..* Resistance from colleagues, few opportunities for promotion, and lack of access to informal social networks have been identified as obstacles.

Betsy, 44, Ph.D., senior program manager, sums up the problem for the many Beyond Superwomen who identified this problem:

Not being part of the "in" crowd of the organization, I have had to work to overcome the resistance from top management. I've had to do more than anyone else to get the same promotions. It has required excessive commitment to hard work and proving my competence to get where I am.

With a Ph.D., I was given an upper middle management position immediately, but my male co-workers really have resented it. They tell me that I haven't earned my place; I haven't "carried the water," so I don't know what the company is really all about. Women resent me too. They call me "Miss Hot Shot" and don't include me in their informal network. The environment I work in can hardly be called convivial or supportive.

4. *Personal barriers.* Research shows that women professionals have had more personal barriers than men. Intense and dedicated to their jobs and careers, Beyond Superwomen approach each assignment with all their energies and skills. They put in as much time and effort as is necessary to complete the task. As a result, they often run into management problems and stress levels created by their own conscientiousness and periodic burnout.

> I can never find enough time in the day to do all the things I need to do. I want to do the best job I can, but I seem to be constantly overloaded with assignments and can never work my way from down under. This is a major problem for me. It makes me feel guilty that I can't produce all that is expected of me.
> After my secretary goes home at the end of the day, I often sit at the typewriter and type my own reports. I know that she is overworked too, so if I can alleviate some of her load, I'll do it. I know this sounds like Superwoman, but I don't want to run her off by making unreasonable demands on her.
> *Adelaide, 55, multiproject supervisor*

> One of my worst problems involves the social and political aspects of the job. I am the only female area director. As a result, I have not attended meetings that would be very beneficial to my career. It doesn't look very becoming for a lady to spend the time at meetings and conventions with male area directors.
> The men don't bother to fill me in on meetings I have missed. Even if I ask them about the meetings, they give me sketchy information. Not only am I not informed, I don't have the benefit of the informal social structure which builds personal bonds between co-workers.
> I think that my career is harmed by not socializing with the guys after work. What can I do? I'm damned if I do, and damned if I don't. Women really have a dilemma. The double standard is a killer.
> *Judy, 48, area director*

5. *Sex discrimination.* Although sex discrimination is illegal, very powerful discrimination still exists in practice. Research shows that it is not limited to female dominant professions.

Sexual prejudice is pervasive and present in just about all the newspapers for which I have worked. I, along with all women, suffer because of the lack of seriousness with which women are treated professionally. I have always spoken up for my co-reporters when I've been aware of adverse situations and have tried to make others aware of assumptions that lay behind their language and behavior.

There is also a prejudice against women journalists who have earned a Ph.D. Editors-in-chief seem to be afraid of people with advanced degrees. As a result, they want to humble you and make you work your way up the ladder by covering areas which have nothing to do with your expertise. For example, I have a Ph.D. in economics, but my first assignment was to cover the courts. It really put my patience to the test to write about subjects in which I had no background.
Della, 45, city editor, daily newspaper

I can summarize sex discrimination in three short sentences:
1. Men are preferred over women for top administrative positions.
2. The community does not accept females as true leaders.
3. Few opportunities are made available to women.
Sheila, 45, staff development director

Although my capabilities are recognized and utilized it has been made clear that promotions, recognition, and higher salaries are reserved for men.
Amy, 55, director of administration

Top leadership roles are still held by males and will continue to be so for some time. This is due in part to the beliefs of the community. Our community feels that women should be teachers, housewives, nurses—roles that are unquestionably female.

If I were starting again, I think that I would like to be a partner in a brokerage firm. But I know that would be a real battle and set off a new array of problems, but I feel that my qualifications would allow me to do a good job.

Yvonne, 42, securities financial analyst

Ann, 44, is a good example of Beyond Superwoman. Intuitive and very perceptive by nature, Ann was able to identify the major obstacles to her career as a budget analyst as early as the age of 23.

"I always have been able to read people very well and knew when people would come gunning for me. As the only woman hired as an analyst in the budget department, I was resented by men and women. Women were vicious gossipers, and the men in the department were even worse. The men continually tried to keep me from getting the exposure and access I needed for my job. They hinted that I shouldn't tour some of the state facilities under my jurisdiction because, 'that is no place for a woman.' They played politics with my supervisor and tried to downgrade my pay scale so that it would be higher for men of comparable rank. They picked at every word in my reports and wanted to find mistakes in my analyses. You name it, they tried it.

"During my first presentation to a top-ranking official, he listened intently to my report and then dismissed it by saying, 'Hell, lady, what you're talking about would be leftovers in our Mulligan stew back home.'"

Ann dealt with that remark the same way she deals with any question. She asked him what he meant by that, and then explained her work factually and objectively. The official, like all her previous critics, never harassed her again.

Using her intuitive and technical skills, Ann has been very successful in identifying and dealing with professional obstacles. She acquired these abilities more through her upbringing than through formal training. She has never taken any courses in management, leadership, interpersonal relations, or conflict resolution.

Ann was born in rural Arkansas and was an only child until her brother was born ten years later. Her father was a building maintenance supervisor and her mother was a teacher's aide. The family was a close one and spent a lot of time together.

"My dad and I were constant companions. I was like a son to him. He taught me to hunt, fish, target shoot; we used to go out in the woods regularly to enjoy nature and get away from the world. I think that's where I learned to be intuitive, by developing keen senses during our outdoor trips.

"During those trips my dad would tell me about his travels and adventures. He had been across the United States by the time he was 21. All those stories inspired me to set out on my own, to be self-sufficient and independent. That was the only way, in my mind, that I could avoid living a dull life in a run-of-the-mill job."

From childhood Ann was encouraged by her parents to get an education and to make something of herself.

"I didn't know what I wanted to do because there were no role models when I was growing up. Women were homemakers, teachers, retail clerks, or nurses, and I didn't want to be any of those." After graduation from college with a double major in accounting and marketing, Ann moved to the state capital to take a job as the manager of a women's apparel shop. After three months, she had evaluated her future with this company and concluded that she would hit a dead end very quickly. So she quit.

Using her family's long involvement and contacts in politics, Ann was hired as a budget officer for a state planning task force which was being created. She set up the books and handled all the accounts for the federally funded state projects. After a year she discovered that she was being paid less than a man of lower rank. She complained, but was told that she had to prove herself. She did. She took the state merit exam in accounting. Of the 50 people who took the test, Ann was the only woman candidate and the only person to pass the exam.

Ann was immediately offered a position in another department. The department in which she was working immediately offered her another position and matched the salary increase.

"Even though I liked the proposal, I told the department head that I would have to think about it. I didn't want him to think I would jump just because he snapped his fingers. My father told me that I shouldn't be so cocky, but Mom encouraged me to hold out just to show them that I couldn't be pushed around.

"I decided to accept the promotion and stay in the same department because that was where all the action was. It took three people to take my place and to do the job I was doing with the task force. I'm telling you, a woman always has to prove herself. She has to fight tooth and nail every inch of the way. Even though a woman is capable, she gets ahead only through hard work."

Ann joined the budget office as the first woman budget analyst and was assigned to help the legislature with the state budget process. Today, with 23 years' experience with the state budget, Ann is a senior analyst. She has survived many administrations and power shifts at the legislature. She is well-respected by all the legislators; the leadership has a high degree of trust and confidence in the thoroughness of her work and the soundness of her recommendations.

Using her skill in judging people, Ann has built powerful alliances with key legislators whom she spotted as potential leaders when they were freshmen. She educated them in the budget process, cultivated their trust, and helped develop a very knowledgeable core of legislators. Consequently, when Ann makes a recommendation, the leadership listens.

Ann has not only overcome the obstacles she encountered in her early career, she also has become a very influential and powerful woman in the state. She is not a household name; she never makes headlines; she is totally unassuming and modest; but the movers and shakers in state government all acknowledge her expertise and her clout as well as their great respect for her.

Individual coping mechanisms

Beyond Superwoman's coping mechanisms and operating style also distinguish her from Hearth Tender and Superwoman. Hearth Tender coped with adversity and problems by being helpless and dependent. Superwoman developed a cheerful, enthusiastic style in her attempt to fill many roles. Both of these stages, as I have discussed earlier, produce very unsatisfactory results interpersonally and professionally because women in them understand neither themselves nor others very well.

Hearth Tender and Superwoman have never realistically analyzed internal and external obstacles that hinder their progress. Rather, they have followed tradition and hoped for the best.

On the other hand, Beyond Superwoman has objectively evaluated the barriers to her career, her chances of success, and her own temperament. Armed with that assessment Beyond Superwoman developed an operating style that allows her to deal more effectively with her professional and personal life.

To a large extent, temperament and circumstances dictate Beyond Superwoman's mode of operating. But the success of any given style depends on the degree of accuracy with which Beyond Superwoman assesses herself and the obstacles she encounters. Success will also depend on Beyond Superwoman's ability to feel comfortable with it. Anything artificial or contrary to her personality will create stress and anxiety and will not last very long.

Sometimes figures in highly visible positions influence leadership style. Part of that style is designed for job and personal effectiveness; part of the style is used to build public image and personality. Many of these character traits are designed to leave an indelible mark in the public's mind and over time become legendary styles.

Lyndon Johnson, for example, created two images through his style: the charmer who was at once disarmingly folksy and decisively persuasive and the Machiavellian leader who always knew how to win or coerce allies and enemies to support his position. Johnson reveled in his public image as a gangling Texan who parlayed his way from a modest rural background into the United States presidency by using his wit, charismatic personality, and ruthlessness.

Ronald Reagan, on the other hand, developed a sincere, reassuring, ceremonial style. He emphasized his high level of delegation of responsibilities rather than his personal involvement with details and strategy. He prefered to be the titular leader, while Johnson wanted to be the leader in fact.

Erstwhile New York real estate wunderkind Donald Trump liked to set the pace and example for his staff which supervised his multibillion dollar operation. He involved himself in minute details and was reported to have even selected paint colors and bathroom fixtures for the the $1 million condominiums in the luxurious Trump Tower in New York. His staff confirmed that he is a workaholic and is fully knowledgeable about the details of his projects. At the same time Trump has developed a flamboyance and high-energy image for the public that was interested in the successful man behind the billions. Trump postured about his unerring business instincts and the level of his profits that measured in the hundreds of millions of dollars. The media dutifully reported his mutterings, and a mythical hero was born.

Movie great Katherine Hepburn built a feisty style which has been cultivated and perfected over her 50-year career. Hepburn's upper-class northeastern background and education at Bryn Mawr served as explanations of her strong-minded, outspoken, and independent syle. Unlike other stars in the early Hollywood era, Hepburn refused to let herself be manipulated by the movie moguls and continued to assert her own personality and values despite studio pressure to give the fans the glamor and gossip they craved. The studios eventually decided to capitalize on Hepburn's real style and personality. Articles about her eccentric independence and and highly private life created a loyal following for decades, and she has been cited by feminists as the first assertive woman who was never cowed by anyone or anything. Hepburn, by being herself—however cantankerous—has proved the long-term effectiveness of her style and personality.

But we average women do not find ourselves in top leadership or highly visible or heroic positions. The careers in which we find ourselves are nevertheless challenging and have great potential for fulfillment and satisfaction. What we need is a set of coping mechanisms which help us accomplish our goals.

Beyond Superwoman has rejected the sweet dependency of Hearth Tender and the boundless enthusiasm of Superwoman. Beyond Superwoman devised a style which incorporated her natural personality and her perception of what is needed to be effective. Ann, the senior analyst, is politically sophisticated. Early in her career she had the benefit of two very powerful mentors who gave her encouragement and invaluable insights into the workings of the political netherworld. They taught her what to look for, what to avoid, how to survive. From that tutelage Ann used her instincts and knowledge to develop a style which is responsible for her success.

"I never play favorites. I tell everyone the same thing; I present my work capably and professionally. I am dependable and never violate anyone's trust or confidence.

"My husband taught me to think globally and not get caught up by small items. He taught me patience, and I think these traits have really helped me mature and become a better analyst and negotiator.

"I am also a very good listener. You can't learn anything if you are talking. My parents always told me that shallow waters make a lot of noise; deep water is still and quiet.

"I think my listening skills and my open approach with everyone—in my job and in the community—have served me well."

People who know Ann agree. In addition to her competence, her style and personality account for much of her staying power and success in the volitile political arena. Her style also carries over into her personal relationships.

Ann is a woman toward whom people have a natural affinity. Her warmth and accessibility lead others to seek her out as a friend, as an empathic listener, and as a source of advice on a variety of personal and job-related problems.

"I think I'm the Ann Landers of state government. Everyone I meet seems to feel comfortable with me, so sooner or later I find myself a confidante of these people. They look to me to give them helpful advice and reassurance. As busy as I am, I always have time to help somebody out.

"I really love people. I guess it shows."

Ann's management style is totally her own creation, without the benefit of graduate business school programs. Her success is due entirely to her own instincts and her keen sense of observation.

Each Beyond Superwoman develops her own coping strategies to adapt to her particular circumstances. Debby, 35, director of corporate human resource development, describes her coping strategies:

> The vice president for personnel is interested primarily in his own self-enhancement, ego building, and control. His interest in and knowledge of people and personnel problems are seriously lacking. He is a blight on the organization.
> My solutions are: (1) I found another vice president who is receptive to personnel needs and morale and has the power to approve my requests; (2) I learned to fight immediately for what is crucial and to wait on others; (3) I always weigh the options of a project, determine who is for it and who is against it and try to minimize my risks.

Winifred, 51, school principal, credits hard work and dedication with her success: "I strive to do my best at whatever task I undertake. This drive for perfection has helped me progress in my profession. Even though I am not perfect, my efficiency and thoroughness have helped more times than not."

Charlotte, 54, a deputy director for a nonprofit organization, soberly assesses her circumstances and resulting style:

> Few positions are available at a higher level, and they usually go to men. So I assume a posture of patience and playing the game. I haven't solved the ethical dilemma of how much I would be willing to compromise my principles and values to get a promotion.
> In trying to overcome the attitudes of men in the organization, I have joined in their group whenever possible, participated in common activities and ignored their actions until I gained their respect for my knowledge and expertise and for the contributions I can make.

Hazel, 63, project director, developed an accommodating technique to get along: "I came along at a time when women were seldom promoted and usually held one position for life. The promotions were reserved for men. The only reason I got ahead is because I was flexible and good-natured. It made my superiors feel I was a real trooper and therefore could be trusted."

From these examples, it is clear that Beyond Superwomen have devised individual styles to deal with their own circumstances. The diversity of their strategies indicates the wide range of behavior, attitudes, and assessments of organizational structures, perceived barriers, and prospects for upward mobility.

Although Beyond Superwomen are not formally trained in socialization models and formal studies of women's work behavior in various organizational structures, these examples of adaptive behavior closely parallel the documented behavioral patterns of both men and women facing similar circumstances.

Rosabeth Moss Kanter's research for *Men and Women of the Corporation* indicates that a woman's work orientation and opportunity for advancement have a greater influence on her operating style and attitude than her being a woman. Kanter asserts that women in low-mobility situations tend to limit their own aspirations and place a greater emphasis on outside activities and interpersonal relationships.[1]

In the case of Beyond Superwoman, where the prospects for advancement are relatively high, morale is high, human relations are generally good, and confidence level is excellent. Beyond Superwoman tends to feel comfortable about the system she has devised for professional success and consequently echoes another one of Kanter's findings: Upwardly mobile managers are receptive to a participatory style in which they share information, delegate, train, and allow autonomy. Conversely, dead-ended managers try to keep control by limiting opportunities for their subordinates and by using coercive techniques.

In summary, Beyond Superwomen came up with their own set of successful strategies based on a combination of intelligent evaluation of circumstances and their best attempts to deal with them. Had Beyond Superwomen gone to business school, they would have learned about theories, research, and prescribed strategies which turn out to be identical to their self-devised operating styles. Through their own acuity and ingenuity, Beyond Superwomen have become quite successful on their own.

Comfortable with responsibilities and power

Using her own skills and her own operating style, Beyond Superwoman is generally quite successful in her career. She has the talent and dedication to excellence which result in extraordinary efforts and initiatives. She is usually very well trained, but she constantly seeks more information about her field so that she can keep up with new innovations, discoveries, and theories in her profession. Consequently, Beyond Superwoman is promoted often in her job and eventually becomes a middle- or upper-middle-level manager. She is comfortable with her responsibilities and power.

As state director of a disease prevention program, Estelle, 59, learned neither how to ascend the organization nor how to gain access to power. What evolved as her style of coping and management developed gradually through trial, error, and temperament.

"I've never thought of success in terms of money or power. To me, it is defined as a job done well and creatively. I have no fear of success, and I am glad to be in an influential policy-making role. This position of prevention director allows me a chance to have a positive impact on the public's health. If I can help create a healthier population, my efforts will have been quite worthwhile."

Clearly, Estelle has neither the the brash ego nor the messianic need for power to save the world. Defined in realistic and achievable terms, Estelle's successes have built on each other and now represent a substantial body of accomplishments. She has the expert and legitimate power through her experience and position to get things done. She doesn't have to use covert strategies like Hearth Tender or Superwoman to get what she wants. But she doesn't seek any higher levels of power. If it happens, it will be fine; if it doesn't, that is also fine.

Estelle is a typical Beyond Superwoman. She did not have a clear set of goals when she started. In fact, while she was growing up in Chicago, she didn't know what kind of profession she wanted.

"All I knew was that I would never be a secretary. Both of my parents worked, but my younger brother and I also felt loved and encouraged. My parents gave us the security and support so that we felt we could be or do anything we wanted. They were very influential in building our sense of confidence and worth. My mother was my role model."

With a master's degree in public health, Estelle's first job 35 years ago was in the male dominated field of rehabilitation. She couldn't fraternize with the male professionals, and the men singled her out in a patronizing way and assigned her to routine jobs.

"For some reason I was not antagonistic toward them even though I knew they were discriminating against me. I was just glad to be learning and working. Even when co-workers made sexual advances,

I tried to ignore those insults rather than be confrontive."

Estelle's even temperament and ability to dissipate hostilities have allowed her to advance steadily with great skill and confidence.

"I am not afraid of success. The level I've achieved is quite satisfying."

Like a Beyond Superwoman, however, Estelle has sought additional training so that she can accomplish more in her job. She has spent the last five years working on a doctorate in public health while working full time. At the same time she has also supported her children through college and taken care of an invalid husband.

"I want to do the best job I can. I am able to juggle many things simultaneously, as my schedule and activities show. I'm happy to have the internal strength to handle these challenging situations as well as my job."

The ease with which Beyond Superwoman handles power at this level distinguishes her from Superwoman, who turns down promotions because she does not want to leave her colleagues and friends and because she does not have enough self-confidence to handle a position with real or perceived power. Superwoman also believes that her friends won't like her any more, if she becomes their boss.

Until recently, power has been very foreign to women because they have not had the opportunity to exercise direct power over themselves or others. In almost all societies in the world, women have been relegated to secondary status. Men have been regarded as more important and, by extension, more powerful.[2] Historically, men have been in charge of governments, armies, and corporations. Women, on the other hand, have been in charge of the home and the children.

Within this limited sphere women learned to influence others and exert what little power they had through interpersonal relationships. That was the only avenue of power opened to them. Paul Johnson, a leading researcher on interpersonal power, defines it as the ability to get another person to do or to believe something he or she would not have necessarily done or believed spontaneously.[3] Hearth Tenders and Superwomen rely on this technique to get what they want.

Until recently, working men and women have had very different responsibilties. Men have been the decision makers and managers, with a clear track to the top of the organization. Women have provided support services which have not led to higher management. Researchers have shown that, as a result of this, there are at least three power dimesnions where men and women differ: (1) direct influence over others, (2) resources they have available, and (3) the degree of competence they stress when trying to exert control.[4] Women traditionally have used indirect power techniques. Instead of asking a person to do something specifically, women have usually tried to get people to do things without actually asking directly. It is a power technique usually associated with people of subordinate status[5] and with women.[6] Psychologists call this technique "manipulation" and contend that women have been trained to use it whenever they need to. They use it throughout their lives. Very few Hearth Tenders and Superwomen move beyond manipulations because they have mastered its use.

Like Martha the Hearth Tender, women have learned from childhood that you can get what you want by buttering up Grandpa, crying when people refuse your request or criticize you, and letting your husband or boss think it was his idea. Behavior which basically conveys powerlessness is counterproducdtive on two counts. First, it creates an oversimplified stereotype of female behavior. It becomes predictable and gender exclusive to women and provides society with a reassuringly easy explanation of "just like a woman." Second, the use of indirect power is effective only in the short run. In the long run it is totally ineffective, since the person who was influenced is unaware of the source of the influence. Therefore, the woman who uses indirect power techniques never gets credit for her influence or power.

Working women who use this technique and who really are the powers behind their bosses rarely get any recognition for their competence, skills, creative thinking, or organizational savvy. The organization and the boss are never aware of these traits, since the source of power is so well concealed. These women are almost never promoted to positions of legitimate power.[7]

Studies show that women who seek to break through the stereotypes and gain access to the inner circles of management have encountered tremendous resistance from society and organizations. In a 1985 *Working Woman* survey of women considered the best candidates for executive positions, half the women were passed over for a promotion at some time, and 65 percent of them felt that gender is a real barrier to further success in the corporate world. These women earned an average salary of $117,000 and were an average age of 39. The image of the Hearth Tender is harder to overcome than anyone would have imagined, especially in a fast-paced society which prides itself on its receptivity to new ideas and products and on its progressiveness.

A second power dimension in which men and women differ is the kinds of resources with which they bargain. Men tend to have more concrete resources, such as money, knowledge, and strength. On the other hand, women use personal resources such as affection and approval. They depend on the goodwill and friendship of others to achieve their goals. Men do not. Through their control of the concrete resources, men can exert, legitimate, punish, and reward power. Women usually exert only referent power.[8]

The Six Bases of Power

Power Base	Typical Organizational Use
1. Reward Power	Power to bestow organizational resources like money, promotions, special privileges, friendship.
2. Coercive Power	Power to withhold or remove organizational resources through demotions, removal of special privileges, hostility, firing.
3. Legitimate Power	Power and authority by virtue of position in the organization.
4. Expert Power	Power achieved through expertise and knowledge.
5. Referent Power	Power achieved through personality, attractiveness or similarity.
6. Information Power	Power achieved by possessing information that others want or need.

Source: Colwill, p. 93

Sarah, 65, typifies those Beyond Superwoman who have used referent power well. She was raised on a large farm in Ohio, one of six children. Her mother was a teacher, and her father ran the farm. The children grew up spending lazy summer days fishing, riding horses, and helping out with the farm chores. They enjoyed the open air and space of their farm which extended to the horizon. The easygoing rural life created a happy, warm environment and a tightly knit family. Each parent contributed to the enrichment of the children and family life. Dad taught the children farm skills and outdoor sports. Mom made sure that everyone grew up with a musical skill and an appreciation for music. Music filled the farmhouse at night after the chores were finished. Everyone either sang or played an instrument, and music became an integral part of family life.

The Depression brought an end to those happy-go-lucky days on the farm. Sarah and her family moved to the city. Life was different and more economically austere, but her parents continued to provide a loving environment and encouraged all the children to set their sights high. The family credo for everyone was that there are no limits to what you can do.

"I know that it was really hard on my parents to feed and clothe such a large family. But somehow we managed. We didn't have much, but still had each other and that seemed to make all the difference. Down deep, we knew that we would be okay in the end.

"When my parents told me that I could do anything, I believed them, I never even knew that there were activities or professions which were not open to women. I just charged ahead. The boys and girls in our family were treated exactly the same, so I naturally thought that the world was like that too."

Sarah was trained to be a nurse. Before she could begin practicing, however, she married Bill. Bill was a bright, ambitious, and very talented architect who had been hired by a big real estate developer to create his dream empire.

Sarah and Bill settled into a very conventional lifestyle established by the social mores of the town. Sarah became a young, social matron who had full-time domestic help to care for the house and children. She became involved with the Junior Red Cross, the local hospital, the woman's club, and the art group.

Coming into a community at the top created immediate jealousy from the local women, so Sarah had to prove that she was worthy of acceptance. Very early Sarah devised a method to counteract the negative comments and actions by the other women.

"It was really hard to be accepted by the people who had lived in town for generations. Newcomers are always suspect. But, you know, we came in at the top so these women had to associate with me whether they wanted to or not.

"Whenever I was asked to do anything, I would seek advice and comments from the other women so that they would know that I valued their experience. I would try to incorporate their ideas into the project. I would never accept a chairmanship or presidency unless one of my detractors was made co-chairman or given a key role. After a while, the local women began to feel that I was okay and accepted me. But it took a great deal of effort to make sure I covered all the bases.

"In the end, I think the community and the causes benefited more from this collective effort than they would have from the divisiveness and jealousy among these women. I'm glad I had a part in putting together effective alliances."

Through a deliberate strategy of seeking advice, Sarah was able to enlarge her circle of firends and supporters and to disarm her enemies. She also never threatened anyone; she was always agreeable. She went along with activities which were expected of women in her social and economic position.

Her personal ability and style of getting along with others account for a large amount of Sarah's success and have led to an expansion of her interests and activities. She was the first woman to run for the state legislature from her district. Although unsuccessful, she set the political stage for women who followed. She was the first executive director of a statewide consumer advocacy organization. She was not there long, but again her activities created a more favorable climate for consumer affairs. She was actively involved in politics and found that "women were not welcomed in the back rooms." However, she worked tirelessly for the party in campaigns, at conventions, raising funds. After years of dedicated work in politics, she was rewarded for her efforts and loyalty. She was appointed as a staff aide to a U.S. senator and later as a state parole commissioner.

"I have always felt the need to pay rent in the world for the life I have had. I need to be involved. I can't name any great achievements other than my involvement in many areas."

Sarah has been a fortunate woman by starting at the top and by hobnobbing with business and political movers and shakers. Her long and distinguished list of activities show the breadth of her interests and involvements. Throughout all of her activities and endeavors Sarah adapted her operating style to disarm those who didn't like her or her causes; she used connections to open the right doors for the causes she advocated. She used her unique personal coping style to accomplish her goals.

How men and women use competence is a third measure of power. Many Hearth Tenders and some Superwomen and Beyond Superwomen use helplessness as a legitimate power base. Rosabeth Moss Kanter found that secretaries in a large corporation were very knowledgeable and articulate about their use of helplessness to get things done.[9] Researchers have found that helplessness does not lead to greater influence and power in a corporation; rather, it underscores the weaknesses rather than the strengths.

Colwill asserts that women who climb up in an organization usually have given up their helplessness and instead have used their competence and direct strategies to move ahead.[10] A study by Rosen and Jerdee confirms this hypothesis.[11] In that study, 100 bank managers took part in a simulated organizational decision about subordinate grievances. This proved that the organizational situation responded more to competence than helplessness.

Ann's position and reputation are the direct results of her extraordinary understanding and expertise in state budgets. She possesses a great deal of expert and legitimate power.

"I feel good about myself and what I know. I admit that I have power professionally, but I never talk about my job in private life. My friends don't even know what I do. All they know is that I work for state government.

"Most powerful women don't show or flaunt it. Most women, however, can't handle power. They think they are God. They feel the only way to be equal in a man's world is to shout about it. They don't know that their strategy does them more harm than good. It turns men off, and it certainly turns other women against them. If these women showed more self-control, they would go farther.

"Power is self-satisfaction—not headlines. Power is accomplishing what you set out to do. For me, it has been extremely satisfactory to help make things better and more equal for the people of this state. Through the budget process, I helped establish a women's equality program and saved taxpayers' dollars by streamlining many state leases, contracts, and management practices.

"I do have power, but I worked for it. I wouldn't want anything I didn't earn."

Kanter feels that professional competence among women in organizations is a given and is not an issue. In addition to their skills and knowledge, women need to be extraordinary, visible, and relevant. Risk taking and high visibility are the two important ways to display extraordinary talent and performance to higher management.[12]

Although scholars and studies have shown that women need to demonstrate a high level of competence and have the ability to control resources in order to move into leadership positions, it has been very difficult to achieve for two reasons. First, many women executives usually are token women in an organization and find that they are isolated from the old boys' club. They have no mentors, male middle managers resent them, no one extends a helping hand, and many are waiting for them to make mistakes. Second, in trying to get along they assume either a solicitous style or a low profile. Both strategies limit their professional and psychological development and adversely affect their chances of being accepted as mainstream leaders. By assuming a low profile, women managers will not have the high visibility they need to impress top managers with their performance. This unobtrusiveness also allows male competitors to keep women in routine dead-end positions in the organization and to pressure them into assuming sex-stereotyped roles.[13]

Because women find themselves severely limited by these factors, they often feel that they are trapped and have no control over their own destinies. The result, then, is a learned helplessness even at high levels. There is a mental and emotional resignation to being ineffective. Seligman found in his studies that people actually stop trying to influence their environments when they conclude that they have no control over what happens.[14]

These token, isolated women in management usually end up playing one of the female stereotype roles forced on them. Most of these roles emphasize the nurturing behavior of women.

The first role is that of mother. She becomes the company mother figure, giving positive reinforcement to other staff members, providing a sympathetic ear, and helping other staffers with the mechanics of their jobs or lives, such as making travel arrangements or restaurant reservations. Psychologist Vivian Travis, a specialist in women's issues, chides women for assuming the role of the warm fuzzy and hot-water bottle: "No one ever promotes a hot-water bottle."

Another role men designate for the token woman is that of the fragile female. Here the woman becomes the object of male attention and protection. Men hover over her and offer help whenever they think she needs assistance. The men who think they are protectors are in fact compounding the stereotype of the helpless woman and isolating her further.

The third role men have women workers assume is an offshoot of the fragile female. This one is the cheerful, bright-eyed amusing pet. Her responsibility is to provide good humor and support for the male efforts and to be cute. Even if she carries out an assignment with a high degree of competence, her efforts are dismissed as "precious." Because she has been the office pet, no one takes her seriously as a professional.[15]

All three classes are trapped and isolated from mainstream interaction and acceptance. It becomes almost impossible to escape the stereotype and become a top-level executive by exerting legitimate power.

Claudia, 63, department director, candidly summarizes the feelings of the token woman:

Many times women executives are hired so that the organization will have a woman to meet the public image. Many men become incensed by this. They are jealous of promotions of women and openly state, "She got that because she is a woman." That woman will not be accepted in a group of men.

As a token woman, I've had to be pleasant, exchange greetings, and smile through such chauvinist remaks as, "You look good today. Let's not go to the meeting. Let's go elsewhere." And guess who is always asked to be the secretary when I am the only woman attending a top-level meeting.

But when there are serious strategy discussions, the men go off and tell me they'll fill me in later—which they never do. Whether it is subconscious or a plot, men continue to band together and treat women as second-class citizens.

Recently, management training has begun to use a two-prong approach to management style to try to break this cycle for women: a more humanistic approach for men because they have been traditionally more task-oriented, and a more instrumental approach for women. This training for men seeks to counterbalance their stereotypical tendencies. The following table shows both male and female tendencies along with the human relations norm.

The prospects for women to gain and maintain power are getting better. The process is sometimes agonizingly slow because of the social and psychological barrirs created over generations. The barriers women impose on themselves by not exercising power and control over their own lives also will require an enormous effort. But clearly this is the starting point for women and power. They will be able to exert influence over others and organizations only when they have taken control of their own lives and feel confident about themselves and their skills.

In his book *Power and Innocence* Rollo May has written that power is necessary in order to have psychological well-being. He asserted that a person has to exert some power and take risks in order to be comfortable with herself. Those who don't take risks, like Hearth Tenders and Superwomen, may be unhappy throughout their lives; they don't control their own lives. Their behavior is prescribed by others and by social customs.[16]

Determines own life. Beyond Superwoman takes charge of her own life. She makes decisons for herself. She is much more honest in her dealings with herself and others; she doesn't assume roles like Hearth

Male role tendency	Human relations norm	Female role tendency
Instrumental leadership; task and power orientation	Learn to express feelings	Expressive leadership, nuturance and support
Analytic reasoning; intellectualizing	Learn to pay attention to feelings	Emotional reasoning; intuition
Generalizing	Learn to speak for yourself	Personalizing
Indentity based on achievement; how others see self less important	Learn to receive and be influenced by feedback	Identity dependent on feelings of others toward self; status traditionally based on relationships
Attention to issues of large systems; in a group, remarks impersonal and indirect	Learn to talk personally, directly to others	Attention to small number of others; in a group, remarks addressed personally to another.
Anger and blame externalized; vengeance sought	Learn to take personal responsibility for own behavior	Blame internalized; difficulty expressing anger
Physical distance; hostility-violence in crowded conditions	Learn comfort with physical contact	Greater comfort with being touched; cooperation under conditions of crowding
Fear of failure in the organizational world; get ahead at all costs	Learn to value human concerns	Ambivalence about success in organizational world
Aggression; competition	Learn to behave cooperatively	Cooperation; support
Exhibit strength; hide weakness	Learn to show vulnerability	Exhibit weakness; hide or repress strength

Source: Kanter, p. 382.

Tender and Superwoman. Beyond Superwoman has progressed beyond the traditional limitations and sex role stereotypes which govern Hearth Tender. She has also gone beyond the many roles Superwoman assumes in her attempt to seek approval and affirmation all the time.

Beyond Superwoman's taking responsibility for her own life can take many forms. It can be very low key and in some cases nonassertive. It can be very deliberate and assertive. Or it could be somewhere in between. But whatever approach Beyond Superwoman uses, she is not marching to a beat dictated by others. She has developed the self-confidence to stand alone if necessary and is willing to defend her position. But Beyond Superwomen try never to be abrasive—some through fear of offending others and some because they know when to pull back and what strategy to use.

Beyond Superwoman is more straightforward because she has a clearer sense of her own abilities and a reasonably healthy sense of self worth. She is usually not depressed or angry. She has had professional challenges and successes. She has developed the ability to roll with the punches.

Ann, the budget expert, has been immensely successful in directing the course of her life. Through her own observations and the help of mentors, she rose steadily to her present position. "My colleagues at work respect my abilities, and I think they also really like me, because they actually seek me out as a friend. I feel very flattered that both men and women regard me as a competent professional and a likable person.

"In my private life, I have a happy, close-knit family. My husband and I and our three children do a lot of things together and have a continuing lively dialogue about everything. And my friends and I also have a good time together.

"My life is rich and very satisfying."

Estelle, too has capitalized on all the opportunities that came her way, and with her easygoing nature, she has been able to get cooperation and collaboration where more abrasive personalities would have failed.

Despite the pressures of her job and family responsibilities, Estelle has always found time and energy to help a feminist project, a political candidate, a good cause.

"My life is busy, but I am a citizen and a human being, too. I am never too busy to lend a hand to a worthy cause or group. This kind of involvement is what life is all about."

Estelle's life is filled with accomplishments and good personal relationships which are the results of her outllook toward life. Even with financial and personal demands that would seem overwhelming to the average person, Estelle is always upbeat and able to meet her daily challenges with an admirable amount of graciousness and an enormous amount of skill and intelligence. Beyond Superwomen represent a major departure from the conventional attitudes and behavior American women have had for generations. In seeking a greater level of satisfaction and challenge for themselves, they have carefully determined the reasons for the long-lasting staus quo and then devised a method to overcome the barriers created by society. In that process, Beyond Superwomen developed a style which allows them to be successful and a self-confidence which enables them to acknowledge and enjoy their success, power, and humanity.

To get to this point, Beyond Superwoman expended a great deal of effort to overcome the psychological and emotional hurdles of convention and to chart her own course. This chapter has shown that Beyond Superwoman has achieved success not only in her profession but also, and more importantly, in becoming independent in determining her own destiny.

The psychological progress achieved by Beyond Superwoman is a quantum leap from Hearth Tender and Superwoman. It is this phenomenal success which gives Beyond Superwoman the ability to work and live with her shortcomings and strengths and to accept responsibilities and rewards for her efforts.

FROM THE FIRING LINE: A CASE STUDY

Teaching, nursing, and social work were the primary professions for many women from the nineteenth century until the last three decades. All three attracted some of the brightest and most dedicated women who wanted careers which were both challenging and fulfilling.

Since these professions comprised such a large component of the women who worked outside the home, their experiences and influences on younger women are very significant. They basically set the stage and created the climate for today's modern woman through their attitudes, adjustments to the demands of work and home, advancement opportunities, and reputation as intelligent and vital professionals.

This chapter is a case study of women in education in North Carolina. And while many will feel that a Southern example of teachers does not apply to women in other fields in other parts of the country, our study and workshops in various parts of the country show that women who straddle Superwoman and Beyond Superwoman in Boston, Detroit, and Los Angeles are no different than Superwomen/Beyond Superwomen in North Carolina. Their reactions and attitudes are basically the same; their levels of interpersonal skills are identical; their insecurities are the same.

In testing our training modules around the country we discovered that our original hypothesis that women differed by region and profession was totally invalid. Just because a woman was a stockbroker or a junior advertising executive did not mean that she was at a higher level of psychological development than a teacher or social worker. We discovered that Superwoman/Beyond Superwoman, no matter what her profession is, possesses common traits which distinguish her from other stages of psychological development.

Susan grew up in a small North Carolina town of 200. Her father was a farmer who had worked the land since he left school at the age of fourteen. Her mother had finished high school but had gotten married right away. She took care of all the light chores around the farm, did the "woman's work" in the house, and raised the children.

In the lush tobacco country and the simple rural life, Susan learned that family and sex roles are clearly defined and very traditional.

Bright, bouncy, and directed, Susan steadily moved up in the teaching profession—from teacher to counselor to assistant principal. Yet with this impressive track record, Susan has a great internal conflict between her ambition and her upbringing.

> Women's biggest enemies are probably themselves. We have not as yet been conditioned to be ambitious and determined (not from birth on, at any rate.) We've had to learn it as we got older. Therefore, it's tougher to fight the obstacles at times. You've got two value systems—one which says, "It's okay, you don't have to do so much—women aren't expected to," and one which says, "The world is open to you; go get it." It's hard work to fight off the old values. You get tired and wonder if it's worth it. But most of the time I know it is, and I keep fighting.
>
> *Susan, 38, high school principal*

Thirty years after the publication of *Feminine Mystique*, the women's movement and women's liberation, the American woman has reaped the benefits of a better self-image and higher expectations. But she is confused and continues to grapple with tremendous internal conflicts about her place and role.

Leaders of the women's movement have helped create a new generation of women who are aware of themselves, their opportunities, their potential. As though the scales had been removed from their eyes, millions of women have discovered a new world—one in which they actually can make a difference if they want to and are encouraged to do so. They have received social sanctions to aspire to become fuller human beings, to be on the cutting edge in almost all professions. The response has been exciting and overwhelming as women have reached out for new directions and expanded roles.

The sky is the limit—or so women are told. Encouraged on all fronts by feminists and by popular magazines, the American woman can become whatever she wants to be. This optimistic outlook has served to boost the morale and ambition of today's woman.

Yet for all its positive effects, these messages have created psychological and emotional turmoil among many women. Women who were raised in the tradition of well-defined roles express a great deal of conflict in resolving their professional ambitions and their personal lives.

Emily's mother played a key role in encouraging her daughter to pursue a career. She worked outside the home while Emily was growing up, so she provided a strong role model for her daughter. There was never any question in Emily's mind that she would become anything but a professional woman.

> I have been married and childless for nearly 12 years. I now wish to have a child but am terrified that if I get pregnant and stay out for the first three months, that will be perceived as not being serious in my goals and aspirations and that it will slow down my advancement appreciably. This is a terrible dilemma. It's difficult for people to believe that you could want both.
>
> *Emily, 32, assistant principal*

Mary started as a classroom teacher and advanced to a general supervisor, then instructional coordinator, and then to assistant superintendent. Along the way, Mary got married and had two children.

> Probably the greatest obstacle any woman faces is marriage; I love my husband and children, but let's face it. I can only accomplish so much. My career has been a series of trade-offs. I don't believe it is possible for any woman, or man for that matter, to give their [all] to a career and to also be fair to a family.
>
> *Mary, 40, assistant superintendent*

Susan, Emily, and Mary express frustrations of being torn by dual messages. Each has been successful professionally, and each has managed a household and family as well. But each woman candidly and painfully expresses her struggle in juggling career and home and trying to do the "right thing" for her family as well as for her employer.

These women are representative of the 450 top women educators studied at the Center for Women in Educational Leadership at the University of North Carolina.

CWEL was established in 1979 on the campus at Chapel Hill to address the problem of access of women to leadership positions in education.

Very few women have risen to the top of any profession in this country. This is true of all fields from public education to business. Given the facts that women comprise 53 percent of the population and 40 percent of the work force, women are distinctly underrepresented in the higher executive levels of every profession.

The problems of advancement for women seem to be exacerbated in the field of education because it is a predominantly female one. For this reason, CWEL's primary focus was on the problems and solutions to the professional progress of educators.

CWEL identified women in North Carolina who were interested in moving into administrative positions and women who were perceived to have leadership potential. These women were invited to participate in exploratory sessions conducted by CWEL staff and consultants. The primary purpose of these sessions was to assess the needs of these potential leaders, their concerns, their ambitions, the barriers they encountered, and to identify psychological barriers they imposed on themselves.

In addition, CWEL surveyed 450 top women administrators to gain more information on the myths and realities about women in the system and to determine both the positive and negative elements which affect the professional decisions and progress of these women.

Many social scientists have spent the last three decades researching the social and historical factors that have contributed to the underutilization of talent, experience, and leadership potential among women. Based on their findings, researchers have proposed remedies to assist women who want to be more fulfilled individuals.

Researchers and feminists have suggested that women need assertiveness training, support groups and networks, affirmative action, child care, and flex time so that they can advance professionally and personally. Presumably, all of these would relieve the stresses produced by the dual messages. Assertiveness training breaks the traditional subservient cycle in which so many women operate. It helps them develop a sense of self-worth, of confidence, of respect for themselves and others. Support groups allow women to share their experiences, triumphs and frustrations with each other, and from that they gain insights, advice, and objective evaluations of their situations. Since women generally have operated in isolation, networking is considered a good alternative to the "old boys' network." Affirmative action, child care, and flex time are self-explanatory and are designed to help women enter the job market on a reasonably equal footing with men. All these remedies are designed to reduce the conflict between feminist and traditional messages.

The results of the CWEL study reveal some astonishing attitudes toward these panaceas; indeed, in a myth-busting tour de force, they also struck down the fear-of-success myth and the Cinderella syndrome.

These women, who have been on the firing line, do not display any fear of the success they have achieved, and unlike women studied in the 1960s, they do not have any mental scenarios of future disasters, because they have already achieved various levels of success. Rather, they showed extraordinarily strong professional goal orientation and were very comfortable with their achievements. And contrary to the theory that all women want to be dependent and taken care of—the Cinderella syndrome—these women did not even mention the thought or entrenchment from their professions to become full-time homemakers. Only one respondent out of 450 indicated that she would quit working if she could financially afford to do so. Not one woman in the study is waiting for a knight in shining armor to rescue her; not one woman expressed resentment about working; everyone elected to have a profession and to remain in it.

To assist women in achieving their professional goals, researchers and active feminists have assumed the women need skills in assertiveness, support groups, affirmative action, child care. As a consequence, untold thousands of women all over the country have attended consciousness-raising courses, assertiveness training, and stress management. Government agencies at all levels and many private organizations have adopted affirmative action policies.

However, the women surveyed in the CWEL study indicated that organizational affirmative action, awareness of affirmative action, and flexible work hours have had no effect whatever on their career progress. In addition, these women feel that assertiveness training and special career guidance have had minimal effects on their professional advancement. They also said that mentors did not have a significant role in their careers.

If these results weren't astonishing enough, the most significant finding was that the dual role of career woman—mother was not perceived as having any effect on their professional progress. Household responsibilities like child care, meal preparation, and housekeeping were not considered by them as hindering factors in the careers of these women.

Women in this study, who have apparently relied on pulling themselves up by their own bootstraps, have said loudly and clearly: they have managed to overcome the mechanical and logistical problems of their dual roles, and they have not felt the need for special courses or special emphasis on their conflict to provide them with coping skills. But they do emphasize that the conflict is there, and it is troublesome to them.

Many indicated in their comments that it was very difficult during the years with young children and career demands, but they all said that it was behind them now. They expressed both pride and relief in dealing with their careers and personal lives so satisfactorily. However, they do not regard themselves as having been particularly courageous or self-sacrificing in the process. No one felt sorry for herself. What we have is an incredible example of women doing what they have always done, that is, doing what they have had to do, with adaptiveness and resourcefulness and often with no emotional support.

Betty was determined to be a career woman. Coming from a modest background, she held part-time jobs to finance her education. When she finally graduated, she started as a classroom teacher and progressed to the rank of associate professor at a college. However, teaching at the high school level remained her first love, and she left college teaching and returned to the public school system. After 30 years in the profession, Betty is now a director of vocational education.

> When my son was born and I decided that I wished to return to teaching, I received a good deal of criticism from my mother. "The women in our family did not work after they had children." For me the decision to return to work was not a difficult one. I knew that I was happier when I was employed outside the home. Today, almost 30 years later, I know that I was a better mother because I did work. My work was a challenge, and it did not get boring. My hardest battle was trying to prevent the guilt that others tried to impose on me.
> *Betty, 52, director of vocational education*

The women attributed their success to (1) a tremendous determination to pursue a career, (2) a sole reliance on personal strength, and (3) sometimes, encouragement and support from family and spouse. Most of the women volunteered that continued spouse support was a crucial factor in their careers. Without the cooperation of their husbands, the vast majority state they would have quit work rather than dissolve the marriage. This should not be surprising if one simply recalls that men in leadership roles also rely heavily on spouse support; indeed, many corporations require that their executives have wives who are committed to their husbands' careers.

On a professional level, these women described themselves as having high motivation, with all the leadership and problem-solving skills and the emotional toughness to be successful. They did not feel that they needed additional social and political skills to advance in their careers.

Asked to determine major obstacles they have encountered, the survey group indicated that the scarcity of promotional opportunities had the most negative effect. Again, surprisingly, these women felt that the following organizational factors have had no negative effects on their career progress: resistance from male colleagues, resistance from female colleagues, rigid hours or demands for extensive overtime, extensive travel, relocation, inability to gain access to the informal social network in the organization.

The lack of support by their managers had minimal negative effects on the careers of these women executives. The emotional toughness they had described as a strong positive element obviously insulated them from negative elements such as the lack of recognition for good work, no coaching to improve performance, lack of support for innovative ideas and undertaking new projects, and even no career counseling or mentors.

The absence of training and development opportunities was not viewed as an obstacle at all.

The only factor which had a mildly negative effect on their careers was an occasional loss of ambition to move higher on the career ladder. This factor is really quite significant, because these women covered the entire range of desire to pursue even higher-level careers. As successful as they are, their responses indicate some ambivalence and hesitation to climb higher and indicate that the dual messages may have worn thin their commitment to career goals. Their responses surprisingly were evenly distributed in all six categories, from absolutely no desire to a definite commitment. If fear of success exists at all, it is relative to additional career advancement, not current status. The important considerations of professionalism and personal fulfillment revealed that these women pursued careers primarily so that they would have a chance to develop and learn new skills and to have an impact on the organization. Greater responsibility, money, and security were reported to be secondary factors. Power was the least important element in attracting these women to pursue higher levels in their careers.

Power workshops conducted by CWEL confirm the survey results. In a series of workshops which involved power role-playing and included hundreds of women, CWEL found that the women felt very uncomfortable "vying" for power and even more uncomfortable when they had power. The psychological separation and alienation from the rest of the group was always too much to bear. The women with the "power" often expressed a wish to forsake the position of power and to ally with less powerful groups.

Participants in these workshops have described power as "lonely," "a terrible place." Power, when explicit and obvious, tends to produce some feelings of discomfort.

Who are these women who appear to have overcome almost all the obstacles to success with no need to resort to popular notions of training and support? These 450 women turned out to be very traditional, mainstream individuals. The composite woman is 43 years old, married, has a graduate degree, has an income between $20,000 and $40,000, and has 1.8 children. She grew up in a two-parent home in which her mother was a homemaker. She received encouragement equally from both parents. Like may American women, she had piano lessons, dancing lessons, and was a Girl Scout. A significant factor in her background is her participation in team sports. Before it was a socially encouraged activity for girls, a disproportionately high percentage—55%—of these executives played team sports while growing up.

Here is a study of successful women who have conventional backgrounds, conventional female careers, and conventional lives as adults. Their career paths and perceptions of both positive and negative elements indicate unequivocally that they do not have the Cinderella syndrome, and they are not afraid of being successful in the waters they have charted.

The strong personal determination and motivation to move ahead is probably the single greatest factor accounting for their success. They dealt with their obstacles as a matter of course and without hoopla. They obviously possess and use those personal characteristics which they were not encouraged to develop as they were growing up: objectivity, self sufficiency, ambition, and strength.

Since these women all came from conventional backgrounds, their success cannot be attributed to extraordinary circumstances. What their success story tells us is that women have the ability to adapt to and deal with an enormous number of obstacles. These women overcame organizational hurdles, dual-career obstacles, and career-family demands with creative flexibility and skill. As long as they had support from their families, these women were able to resolve the lack of support from supervisors and co-workers. They felt that they did not need networks, affirmative action, or assertiveness training to deal with their problems.

The traditional female profession—education—and the traditional backgrounds of the survey respondents indicate quite strongly that the stereotyped profile of the American woman may indeed not be the mainstream but an aberration.

But all is not the sweet smell of success. Despite the great success professionally and personally, despite the overall balanced approach to life, comments from these women indicate that they are still struggling with the multivalue system and trying to come to grips with it satisfactorily.

> Peer pressure can be quite taxing at times. Today, most of my friends have retired. I am not ready to retire. Someone is always trying to get me to do this or that socially that I cannot possibly do as long as I am employed full-time. Then when I do not do it, they try to make me feel bad because I am still working. I tend to be a rather decisive person, and once my mind is made up I stick with it, but the barbs do get annoying at times.
> *Jane, 58, assistant superintendent*

In addition, these women have paid a price for their success. It is the same price men have had to pay when they have a consuming commitment to their success: less leisure time and less time for personal relationships.

The American woman today truly has many opportunities and choices open to her, and the number of successful women interviewed in the CWEL study shows that they are taking advantage of this favorable climate. The problems of being a professional and a mother have not been major deterrents. The organization and attitudes of men have not been detrimental. But the psychological conflict between the concept of the "new" woman and the traditional values is ever-present in the minds of most of these women and does not seem to be going away.

All the pep talks in the world—about being a modern, liberated woman who can assume so many roles—are not working. Women would like to believe what they are being told but they are frustrated when they try to fulfill them. They are bright, attractive, well-educated, and armed with the tools to set the world on fire.

What the CWEL study found was that women want to and can set the world on fire but have not yet fused the new values with the traditional ones. Consequently, there is a high degree of internal conflict even at this very high level of personal development and consciousness. What women now need to understand is that they indeed can be a professional, mother, sex symbol, fashion plate, and community leader, but not all at the same time.

The aspirations and sights raised by the feminist pioneers were unquestionably beneficial and necessary, but what women need now is a more realistic approach to help them feel more comfortable with their roles and their ability to resolve their personal emotional and psychological conflicts.

Stage IV:
Boat Rocker

The spirit with which the United States was originally founded has changed a great deal. Although, our country was established by revolutionaries who were fiercely determined to assert their independence and direct their own destinies, Americans today seem to be less actively involved and concerned about policies and laws which affect their lives. Instead, citizens seem to be more interested in fulfilling their personal goals than in defending the public's interest.

Everyone seems to want to be part of middle America and its traditions and to have a good life. The prevailing rule has become "get along by going along." It doesn't mean that the country will not rally around a national emergency or crisis, because it will. It does mean, however, that in normal times there is a live-and-let-live attitude that serves as an unwritten rule of behavior. It is therefore understandable that any attitude which challenges the status quo automatically becomes suspect and is held at arm's length.

To many the term *Boat Rocker* is synonymous with troublemaker. It is used to identify the malcontent who is always complaining and finding fault with the world and how it is run. It is generally used to describe someone who will never get ahead because he or she doesn't know how to play the game and is too naive to understand the realities of the system. Boat Rockers are viewed as strange people who march to a different drummer and will be left behind. Others—the majority— feel that they will be better off if they don't rock the boat.

This chapter deals with women who fall into the Boat Rocker category. The discussion centers around the efforts of these women to overcome opposition and criticism in order to achieve their goals, but more importantly, around the personal traits and development of the women who fall into this category.

Exactly what traits set these women apart from other women in other stages of psychological development? Were they single children of parents who married late in life? Did they marry older men who served as their mentors? Did they grow up in progressive urban settings where role models of highly successful women were visible and accessible? Did they grow up in rural settings where both men and women were equal because they share the responsibilities of running a farm?

What emerged from the interviews for this book was the fact that Boat Rockers come from every kind of background and no single factor was more important than others in determining the course these women ultimately chose. They come from all backgrounds: urban, rural, single child, large family, professional mother, homemaker mother, educated parents, undereducated parents, early marriage, late marriage.

Boat Rockers developed a set of common characteristics at an early stage in their lives and careers. By and large, Boat Rockers are distinguished from women in other stages because they have clear goals. They all have specific goals which they have set for themselves and an unwavering determination to pursue and achieve them. They also are keenly aware of the obstacles and problems facing women when they follow untraditional paths and display "unfeminine" ambition.

With a good understanding of the obstacles and criticisms they have encountered and will continue to meet in the future, Boat Rockers generally have made a conscious effort to move away from the passive, submissive Hearth Tenders, beyond Stage II Superwoman and Stage III Beyond Superwoman. That effort was probably precipitated by early disappointments and failures that were substantial enough to cause these women to take stock of their modus operandi and to determine ways to avoid these setbacks in the future.

To get to this level of development almost all of the Stage IV Boat Rockers have learned to be assertive, have developed stress management techniques, have taken leadership training, and have sought support systems and networks. They feel that they can no longer use just what was right for themselves individually to pull themselves up by their own bootstraps. That would not be enough if they wanted to achieve their goals. They also feel that they cannot achieve their goals by themselves. Consequently, they seek help and affiliation with other women to foster mutual growth.

The awareness, training, and networks have combined to give Boat Rockers the confidence and self-esteem to assume responsibility for the major decisions and actions that affect their lives. They are now comfortable enough with themselves so that they don't feel threatened by others, especially other women. As a result, they seek out leadership roles which women in earlier stages of development would not dream of undertaking. The differences lie in the fact that Boat Rockers have no fear of power or success and have enough self-confidence to undertake risks and challenges.

The last and most important trait that Boat Rocker possesses is a successful and honest personal life. As an assertive woman, Boat Rocker usually has been very successful in her personal relationships. Her honesty and respect for others is usually reciprocated. Her self-esteem allows her to acknowledge her limitations and to stand alone when necessary.

Clear goals. Most professional women set long-range goals in their minds, but Stage IV women go beyond that. They establish timetables and schedules for assessing achievement. They acquire the skills and experience they need to attain their goals, and they are relatively circumspect about evaluating their strengths and weaknesses.

Some Boat Rockers begin with their lifetime goals in mind, but many begin with amorphous ambitions that become increasingly well defined through experience and personal development.

Miriam, 36, started with clear goals:

> I have been very fortunate. I am extremely goal oriented. I have wanted to be a school principal since college age. I became an assistant principal at the age of 25 and a principal at 28. Needless to say, I haven't had any real obstacles.
>
> The things that have helped me achieve my goal are: personal leadership qualities, willingness to move, support of my spouse, personal ambition, and a love of what I am doing.

Evelyn, 42, could have been the prototype for the Boat Rocker:

> The greatest factors which have contributed to my career progress are (1) deciding what direction or area to go into, and (2) setting up long-range and short-range goals.
>
> Once these goals were established, I identified strategies that would help me achieve my goals. Career progress depends a lot on self-motivation and identifying early whether or not your personal life can accommodate career goals. Constantly looking for opportunities and exposure (talent, social, political, etc.) also increases career progress.

A person must be willing to devote a lot of personal time and must really like her work. Knowing the organization structure also helps.

You can't be easily intimidated—hang tough when necessary!

On the other hand, Emma, 35, evolved more traditionally. She had no specific goals and still doesn't want any more power than enough to get the job done. Because of her background, she feels fortunate to have opportunities which tap her skills but wants to protect herself from regressing.

Emma is the executive director of a non-profit advocacy organization. To get to this point Emma has worked very hard to consciously move beyond the passive, submissive environment in which she was raised. As an only child of a widow, Emma learned to be independent at an early age. She helped clean the house, do the laundry, and cook before she was a teenager because her mother worked on an assembly line to support them both. By the time she entered college, she could handle almost any situation and was totally self-sufficient. She had grown up with a life script which said, "If I want something, I have to do it for myself."

Emma worked during college to supplement her scholarship. She also helped her boyfriend David as well. When David didn't have enough money for meals, Emma would either cook or buy his meal tickets at the college commons. Emma felt good about being able to help someone else; she felt David gave her moral support, she was no longer alone. She could count on someone else.

David and Emma were married right after graduation, and Emma worked to put David through law school. She became everything to please David: breadwinner, housekeeper, soul mate, and sex object. She waited on him hand and foot, and when he complained that she wasn't earning enough, she took a second job.

David is an idealist and a very honest, good man. He would never knowingly hurt anyone and would never do anything contrary to his values. But as an only son, he was pampered when he was growing up, and consequently never learned any of the skills needed to survive in everyday living. He couldn't do any household repairs, didn't know how to do laundry, never washed dishes, and never learned how to use any tools.

It became Emma's responsibility to take care of all of the household chores and repairs, car maintenance, yard work, cooking, and cleaning in addition to her job. "I was Wendy. David was Peter Pan.

He was the eternal child, and I was more than willing to do whatever I could to help him. Boy, when I look back, I was really stupid."

Emma was not stupid. She did what she did because of her background. Growing up in a small town where very few girls even finish high school before they get married, Emma decided that she would never be trapped into that kind of life. She would never stay in that factory town; she would never marry one of the assembly line workers; she would never perpetuate yet another generation where the only prospect for life is to have a brood of children and play bingo on Saturday nights. She wanted more for herself in her life, and she would find it.

David was one of the ways out.; He was highly intellectual, and Emma delighted in learning and exploring new disciplines just as fast as she could. This new world was where she wanted to be. David was an anchor for her—a stability she had never had before. She belonged with David and his family, and it gave her a great sense of security.

Then, after ten years of marriage, Emma realized that she was still supporting herself and David financially and emotionally. David would resign from jobs if he felt that he was compromising his values. He knew Emma would take care of everything, and she did. Suddenly Emma acknowledged the rage that had been building for ten years: David had taken advantage of her! She had catered to his every whim and neglected her own professional development because they needed a steady paycheck every month. She has always had confidence in her abilities, her talents, and herself, but she felt it was more important to be a supportive wife so that David would fulfill his dreams. She was Superwoman, so the time never seemed right for Emma to quit her clerical job to seek a more challenging position.

Exceptionally bright, Emma excelled at her job in a government agency. She learned the ins and outs of the bureaucracy and was able to get her paperwork approved faster than any of her colleagues. Even in her administrative role Emma had shown her abilities. Her responsibilities increased, and she received incremental raises and promotions. But this was not even close to Emma's ultimate goals.

One day a friend offered her a position as the associate director of a nonprofit advocacy group at a staring salary that was far less than she was making in her government job. But she wanted the opportunity to grow professionally, so she took the position. After a year, the executive director left, and Emma was named acting director.

Emma needed new challenges in her life at that point. Her marriage had begun to deteriorate very fast because she realized that she had always given David moral support and never received any in return. She was tired of holding their marriage together. Emma decided to restructure her priorities and to use her energies and skills to help herself for a change.

The association was more than she bargained for. Plagued with financial difficulties and a feuding board of directors, the organization was just a step away from its demise. Friends advised Emma to leave while there was still some semblance of an organization, but she felt this was a chance to rebuild organizationally and financially. She took it as a personal challenge and was determined to use her skills to do a successful job.

An idealist of the generation which protested the Vietnam War, Emma always wanted to make a contribution to mankind. Now, in her present position, she has the opportunity.

The organization has a history of chewing up and spitting out executive directors, so Emma has a twofold challenge of not only establishing financial stability but also gaining the confidence and support of the board. So far, she has survived. She has survived board presidents who have attacked her work, her performance, her management style. She has survived by building important alliances with influential members of the board and by doing such a competent job that the board is developing confidence in her.

An attractive woman with an irrepressible sense of humor, Emma has set her goals on becoming all that she can be. She has taken risks by leaving both a secure job and marriage so that she can grow. She has been adept at organizational dynamics and played internal politics successfully. She is an assertive, self-confident woman who feels that she has just begun. She does not feel threatened by the success of other women and is savvy enough to spot phony feminists who will stab her in the back at the first opportunity.

Her anger about David's dependence and inability to be emotionally supportive has subsided, and she can now laugh about her ten years playing Wendy to David's Peter Pan. She is slowly working on building more mature relationships with men.

Her organization is still struggling. The board is still erratic, but Emma is still there toughing it out.

What will happen to her and the organization? It is hard to say, but one thing is certain. Emma will continue to grow and to survive primarily because now she has a very realistic view of her life and her own skills. She has the independence and self-confidence so important and necessary to continue to grow.

Miriam, Evelyn, and Emma are just three examples of Boat Rockers who have set goals for themselves. To many people, especially men, it seems obvious that everyone has goals. Why then is it so remarkable that these high achievers have these characteristics?

Clarity of goals is especially important for women. As studies have shown, women generally flow with the tide and are grateful for any advancements or success. Martha McKay, a leading feminist in the South and founder of the Women's Political Caucus in North Carolina and management consultant with AT&T for many years, says that most women don't know what they want to get out of their lives or their careers because they simply won't take responsibility for themselves. They prefer to perpetuate their socialized behavior in their inability to take risks, delegate power, be independent. As a result, McKay asserts, most women don't set up goals and assessments of the time and costs to achieve these goals. The stories of women in Hearth Tender, Superwoman and Beyond Superwoman reinforce what McKay and many psychologists have hypothesized and researched.

As psychologist David Campbell said, "If you don't know where you are going, you'll probably end up somewhere else." In his book with the same provocative title, Campbell, a specialist in career guidance, asserts that if you want something to happen in your life, you have to make space for it.[1] It doesn't guarantee that you will reach your goals just because you establish them. However, you always need to be realistic about their probability of success and what you need to do to increase that probability. On the other hand, you also need to be mentally prepared for failure, because plans can and do fail.

Campbell suggests that goals cover different time spans. Long-range goals deal with the overall style of life you want, such as the type of job or the kind of family you would like to have. Medium-range goals cover approximately five years and cover the next step in your career and may include acquiring additional skills. Short-term goals can cover one month to one year. These goals can be quite achievable if they are realistic.

The time spans used as benchmarks are invaluable in assessing whether or not you are on the right track, whether your goals are achievable. Periodic review allows you to modify plans or to plan for gradual improvement. This method helps avoid catastrophic disappointment.

Boat Rockers have a clear idea of what they want to achieve—vice president, chief executive officer, neurosurgeon, cover girl, governor, congressman, actress. But they also all work to acquire the experience, knowledge, and skills to become more competent and competitive.

Acquire interpersonal and management skills. Most women know in the back of their minds that they have to put in more effort than men in order to succeed professionally.

Betty, 50, summed it up:

> Women are not given the same type of recognition for a job well done as men. Our superiors tend to take credit for the work done by a woman under their direction. They tend to let a male at the same level take credit for what he does. Old-fashioned conservative communities expect men to be in high-level positions—not women.

Even younger women like Mabel, 37, have experienced obstacles despite the feminist movement:

> It is very difficult for a woman to juggle a career as a mother, wife, professional and student. Society has a mold into which women must fit, and there is no room within that mold for the many roles a career woman must play.
>
> Administrative and executive positions seem to be of the male gender. I have had to work twice as hard for half as much in promotions and recognitions. I just continue to hang in there with the best of them.

To counteract the negative responses to their efforts and the constant uphill struggle professionally, Boat Rockers realize early that they not only have to be competent in their profession but they also have to acquire knowledge and skills in two important areas: behavioral skills, which include overcoming self-discriminatory behavior, dealing with self feelings and attitudes and those of others, and coping with the informal system of organizations; and technical skills, which include basic management tools and a firm grasp of organizational dynamics.

Learning to be assertive is the most important step in overcoming low self-esteem and lack of self-confidence and mastering the ability to interact and communicate effectively and satisfactorily with others. Like any other skill, assertiveness is not something you learn immediately. You learn it a little bit at a time. You gradually polish these skills.

One of the essential components in gaining self-esteem is the confidence gained through being assertive. Assertiveness deals with initiating your own goals, having a strong sense of personal identity, independent thinking, and a set of integrated values. It is these values that give assertive people their goals and directions in life, because they are an extension of themselves. They accept their strengths and weaknesses; they acknowledge that they can and do make mistakes; they know that they will have differing views from others; they know that others will be hostile to them from time to time.

Assertiveness in women is still probably one of society's most maligned and misunderstood behaviors. Many people confuse assertiveness with aggressiveness. Women who stand up for their rights or have a different opinion are often accused of being aggressive and castrating bitches.

In all fairness, it should be pointed out that assertiveness is effective only when women understand goals and problems. If women in other stages of development, which are generally nonassertive, try to be assertive, it can do more harm than good.

Assertiveness does not work well for women who are Hearth Tenders, Superwomen and Beyond Superwoman because they very often cannot differentiate the appropriate situations in which to be assertive. Since they have no clear goals, there are also no clear distinctions between priority issues and unimportant ones. They can't distinguish the situations in which they should be honest and express their opinions and those when it is wiser to remain silent. As a result, many nonassertive women who have been exposed to assertiveness training don't use the skill properly. They simply tell everything they know and are feeling because they think they are dishonest if they don't. That trait, as McKay points out,[2] doesn't go over very well in an organization. All it does is to underscore how naive the woman is.

However, once the women figure out what they want and can establish goals, they need to learn how to be assertive, how to take risks, how to deal with power. All of this takes time and a conscious effort. It seems alien and almost "masculine" to women when they are first exposed to it. But with proper training and practice women can master these crucial interpersonal skills and blend them with characteristics often identified as "feminine" caring, concerned, nurturing, warm, and helpful. (See Appendix A for a short description of assertiveness, an assertiveness inventory, and a list of books written on the subject.)

Women have been taught to suppress their true feelings from the time they were little girls, so it is little wonder that most women are nonassertive. Assertiveness training enables women to accept and assert their true feelings, not what they want to feel, or what they think they should feel, but what they actually do feel.

Like Carol the TV anchor woman in the Superwoman chapter, nonassertive women absorb their feelings because they think they are disagreeable if they express their emotions. Even though Jim had made Carol wait for over an hour without an explanation, Carol did not even mention her annoyance. She rationalized that she didn't want to make an issue out of it.

What nonassertive people are telling others is, "I don't count; my feelings don't matter; I am nothing; you can take advantage of me." Nonassertive people ignore their own feelings and rights. Nonassertive women express feelings, ideas or goals in a very indirect manner. Anger is rarely expressed. The behavior is excessively people-oriented. They are so concerned with being pleasing and nice to everybody, they allow others to stomp all over them and to violate their rights. They are passive, compliant, agreeable, and try to avoid conflict at all costs.

Nonassertive people are so preoccupied and concerned about being accommodating and adaptable that they are always followers, never leaders. Consequently, they rarely achieve great success.

The behavior of nonassertive people will be viewed by others as ineffective and will generate feelings of disgust. People who are nonassertive will feel "used" and resentful because others are violating their rights. Anger develops but is turned inward on themselves.

Nonassertive behavior is also manipulative. By acting helpless and dependent nonassertive people get what they want without asking directly.

Why are some people nonassertive? Often they mistake assertion for aggression and don't want to become the "bitch queen." Often they think nonassertive behavior is polite. They don't contradict others or stand up for their rights because they are afraid of hurting someone else's feelings. When they finally blow up and do hurt someone's feelings, they feel guilty about it. Often they think they will be rewarded for being nice and cooperative all the time. Women especially were taught that the world responds favorably to those who are cheerful and supportive and responds negatively to those who have a foul temper and disposition. Often nonassertive people feel that there will be negative consequences if they stand up for their views, rights, or accomplishments. And sometimes, they just may not know how to act otherwise. Assertiveness is so opposite to their upbringing that they cannot conceive of that behavior.

Millions of people are nonassertive and seem to function quite well in the world. Why then is there an urgency to transform them into assertive people? What you don't know doesn't hurt you, right?

Wrong. People pay a very high price for being nonassertive. It costs them their own integrity. It means either a loss of self-esteem or an undesirably low level of self-respect. It means increased disappointment and internalized anger. Ultimately it means great depression.

All of these consequences of nonassertiveness are quite damaging to an individual and her ability to be fully satisfied. It stifles growth, achievement, and happiness. It is emotionally dishonest, inhibited, and self-denying.

The other end of the spectrum is aggressive behavior. Aggressive people have a need to dominate and to win all the time. They achieve their goals at the expense of others and have little consideration for the rights of others. They are excessively task-oriented and seem to be insensitive to the consequences of their actions.

Aggressive behavior has often been explained as the inability to deal with an overload of hostile feelings. It is the determination to achieve one's goals at the expense of others.

Aggressiveness is usually rewarded when men use it and punished when women use it. The only type of aggressive behavior which is permitted of women is passive/aggressive behavior—catty, back-stabbing, indirect aggression.

Below is a chart summarizing the three types of behavior (Alberti & Emmons, 1970).[3]

NONASSERTIVE BEHAVIOR	ASSERTIVE BEHAVIOR	AGGRESSIVE BEHAVIOR
Actor	*Actor*	*Actor*
Self-denying	Self-enhancing	Self-enhancing at expense of others
Inhibited; Does not achieve desired goals	Expressive; May achieve desired goals.	Expressive; Achieves desired goal(s) by hurting others
Allows others to choose for him	Chooses for self	
Hurt, anxious	Feels good about self	Chooses for and depreciates others
Acted upon	*Acted upon*	*Acted upon*
Guilty or angry.	Self-enhancing	Self-denying. Hurt, defensive, humiliated
Depreciates actor	Expressive	
Achieves desired goal at actor's expense	May achieve desired goal(s)	Does not achieve de-

Boat Rockers are assertive through training and experience and are able to choose when to be assertive.

Emma, for example, elected not to vent her pent-up hostility and frustrations about her marriage to David. When she decided to leave David, she told him she was tired of trying and needed to live her own life. She did not tell him about the years of hurt and humiliation she had absorbed. She felt that it would not accomplish anything to further devastate David by telling him how miserable he had been to her all of those years.

By acknowledging her feelings but choosing not to express them, Emma is still an assertive person. If, on the other hand, she could not choose for herself but allowed herself to be pushed into nonassertiveness or pulled into aggressiveness, her life would still be governed by others.

One of the primary benefits of assertiveness is the development of self-confidence and self-esteem. Women who are Boat Rockers generally have what is called "true self-esteem." At first glance the term true self-esteem seems to be pompous and pedantic. By itself the term conveys a strong sense of superiority and snobbishness that would turn any reader off. However, "true self-esteem" is used in a psychological context and will be used in this chapter when discussing the different levels of self confidence.[4]

True self-esteem is probably the one major trait which sets Boat Rockers apart from other women and enables them to take big risks. True self-esteem is based on a sense of worthiness and gives people the confidence to make decisions and accept both the successes and failures of those decisions.

People with true self-esteem have a strong sense of personal identity and well-defined goals and values. Barring the quirks of fate, they make decisions which affect the direction and quality of their lives. This approach sets them apart from people with pseudo or minimal self-esteem because they are not afraid of taking risks or of making mistakes. They know that their opinions and actions may bring them into conflict with others, but they are willing to assume the consequences and responsibility of judging and thinking for themselves.

A healthy self-esteem allows people to deal with their errors, to laugh at their own foibles, to understand their limitations, and to take chances. They even deal with losses philosophically.[5]

Take Mary, for example. She had been a highly successful chief capital correspondent for United Press International and had distinguished herself in breaking more big state political stories than any other reporter. After many years in this position, Mary decided, at age 40, to leave the rat race and to become a public relations consultant. Her ability to quickly evaluate her client's needs and determine the kind of media campaign which will reach the client's goals made her instantly successful in this new business. But her male clients often feel uncomfortable with her abilities.

Recently, a national organization wanted Mary to put together a total fundraising package for its corporate solicitation drive. Mary assessed the need in a matter of minutes and then began to outline the weaknesses of the previous public relations and fundraising attempts and how to build a more positive image. The executive director of the organization went back to his board of directors and said that Mary was inappropriate for the job because she was too aggressive.

Mary was perfect for the job, but her competence and forthright style made the executive director feel threatened and uncomfortable. Because he had doubts about his own abilities and self-worth, there was no way he could hire Mary. He felt that the high quality of her work would make him look inept. The result was that Mary didn't get the job, the executive director put together his own package, and no money was raised. Mary shrugged it off.

Mary didn't magically become mature. It was a long, arduous process in developing self-esteem, It was earned the hard way.

Mary took a long time to acquire true self-esteem. A journalist who has enjoyed a remarkable career and reputation, Mary hardly displays the passive and weak traits associated with minimal self-confidence.

"I always knew I was a good reporter, but I also knew that I had not developed the soft, retiring, and dependent female traits traditional society rewards in women. As a young reporter, I could never seem to make friends with other women cub reporters. They were more interested in their social lives and dressing well than in working 100 hours a week on the paper to build an outstanding career. I was the outcast, so I always felt I wasn't as feminine or appealing as they were. At least that's how I felt at the age of twenty-two. Now I know better and let my personality carry me through. But when you're young that kind of feeling of inferiority can really shake your confidence."

Mary had always been an achiever since she was a child. Growing up with three brothers, she developed competitive as well as team player traits which would stay with her for the rest of her life. There were no concessions to her just because she was a girl. She had to earn respect, compete, and survive in the world of little league baseball, hiking, and camping. In addition, her mother wanted her little girl to learn all the niceties, but the piano and dance lessons were eclipsed by the dirt and dust of sandlot ball and the rigors and excitement of competition.

Even though she had always lived in small towns in upstate New York, Mary was convinced that her physical and mental energy and intensity would provide the necessary qualities to succeed in the big city. So, armed with a brand new B.A. in psychology, Mary headed off to New York City to seek fame and fortune as a budding journalist.

She talked her way into a cub reporter position with *Newsweek* and quickly proved that she had both the scoop mentality and the instincts to ferret out good stories and to beat out veterans in breaking headline articles. In two short years she was well on her way to establishing a national reputation for top-notch reporting.

At the age of 25 Mary received an offer from United Press International to become a capital correspondent in the Midwest. Since she had always had a fascination with politics, she accepted. She spent the next 12 years covering political intrigue and legislative activities.

She once got so close to uncovering major embezzlement by a state official, her life was threatened by organized crime. "They followed me wherever I went. They tapped my phone. They tried running me over a couple of times. They broke into my apartment. But the police were never able to trace it back to the crime bosses."

With an insatiable taste for adventure and a certain pride in taking on the "mob," Mary thrived on being a target. "It comes with the territory. When they start attacking you, you know that you're on the right track. Sure, I was scared when I saw a car coming right toward me. I never ran so fast in my life."

The support she received from the older reporters, all men, gave her the courage to continue with the nitty gritty world of politics and the underworld. She seasoned in a hurry and forgot her insecurities of being less feminine than her mother had wanted her to be. "Boy, the last straw was the mob's attempt to publicly embarrass me. They created a photograph with my face attached to this voluptuous nude body. That was a hoot. Anybody who knew me knew that was the best piece of fiction to be created in a long time!" she laughed.

Mary's continued success as a top reporter in a national political hotbed increased her confidence in herself as a person and as a professional. Awards in journalism reaffirmed her excellence as a reporter, and full acceptance by the capital corps reporters gave her a feeling of belonging. She was one of the gang. She hung out with the "guys" after work, went drinking with them, played cards with them. They were her family, and when she wasn't working 14 hours a day, she was with them.

A vivacious woman who talks at a rapid-fire rate, Mary can and does charm or intimidate anyone at will. She is bright, enthusiastic, and exceptionally well-informed on a wide range of subjects. She also has developed a persuasive and winning style and excellent interpersonal skills. As a result, people take to her naturally. Her naturalness and respect for others allow people to feel comfortable with her almost immediately.

Over the years, Mary developed a style and attitude which allowed her to let defeats and personal insults slide off her back. She knew that she was good in her profession, and she knew that people in general liked her. She had never compromised her values, and realized that she could never be all things to all people. This attitude led to a healthy sense of self-esteem and confidence in herself.

In his book, *The Psychology of Self Esteem*, psychiatrist Nathaniel Branden states that most adults do not have true self-esteem.[6] Instead, most have either pseudo self-esteem or minimal self-esteem. People with pseudo self-esteem appear to be self-confident on the surface, but they deliberately avoid situations that make them feel inadequate or inferior. Rather, they seek a sense of worth through "doing one's duty," financial success, or sexual attractiveness. Reality on all levels is a threat to them.

People with minimal self-esteem are anxious, insecure, and feel incompetent. Like the Superwoman, many women try to please everyone in order to feel worthy and in order to live defensively and safely. Afraid, self-conscious, and self-protective, Superwoman selects a lifestyle which will minimize her risks and prospects for failure. The supermom wants her children to adore her in exchange for the sacrifices she makes for them. The corporate wife validates her identity through the success or failure of her husband. The sex symbol relies on her glamorous image of herself to avoid reality. She engages in romantic relationships with any man to assure herself that she is desirable and lovely. She represses the humiliation and her fear of growing older. Her ego is so fragile that she needs constant and fresh admiration.

When Superwomen don't win approval all of the time, they feel rejected and have only a minimal sense of self-worth. Psychiatrist rejected and have only a minimal sense of self-worth. Psychiatrist Helen DeRosis has indicated in her work *The Book of Hope: How Women Can Overcome Depression* that women make unrealistic demands on themselves and irrationally judge themselves even though they know that they can't be perfect. Yet they keep trying, and when they fall short, they feel incompetent and guilty. They feel miserable; they have less energy; and finally, they become depressed and helpless. They are suffering from a self-esteem crisis. No life-threatening situation exists; there is no impending peril. Yet they feel threatened and anxious. Branden states that pathological anxiety leads people to feel impotent and to imagine both disaster scripts for themselves as well as an overwhelming sense of guilt. This anxiety is the direct opposite of self-esteem and confidence. It is the mental creation of the person suffering from lack of self-esteem and has very little to do with her real-life situation.[7]

The greatest failure of a woman who lacks true self-esteem is the inability to assume intellectual responsibility for her own existence and the fear that she will make mistakes. By not thinking or making judgments for herself, she is forced into positions of being dependent. She chooses not to make decisions based on her own evaluations and convictions and consequently chooses not to mature. She doesn't want to contradict others, so she goes along with them.

This social metaphysical fear creates paralysis. It is a total dependence on others. It is a decision to live within the rules established by others. A woman with this fear is a psychological parasite because she doesn't want to make any decisions on her own. She is afraid that her decisions might show that she is inadequate or unworthy. She believes that others control reality; she feels helpless and afraid because she doesn't know how to deal with objective reality. She substitutes the consciousness of others for reality, and her pseudo self-esteem depends on acting in accordance with what others believe to be true and right. The approval she gets from others becomes her proof of worth.

By giving in to this social fear, this insecure woman elects not to think, not to choose her own values, not to assume responsibility for judging what is right or wrong, true or false, and not to assume responsibility for her own life.

Emma allowed David to take advantage of her because she had a low self-esteem during her college years. David confirmed Emma's wretched view of herself and condescended to love her even though she was so unworthy.

"I was so grateful that David 'let' me love him. I did everything for him. Anything he wanted...."

Whenever David treated Emma with contempt, the more it confirmed her self-effacing perception. He could reduce her to tears with a sneer; he could humiliate her with a comment. "He enjoyed feeling dominant and superior and enjoyed playing psychological games with my emotions. He didn't do it knowingly, but had a need to feel superior, and I was easy prey."

It was not until Emma started working that she discovered that people liked her and that she had important skills. Co-workers responded to her comic personality and her caring nature. Emma began to develop self-confidence, but it was usually eroded by David at home. His strength and superiority always won out at Emma's expense.

It took years of affirmation of her work from the outside world before Emma finally decided that she was really an extremely competent and likable woman. At that point, she began her withdrawal from the morbidly dependent relationship she had with David. She began to define herself, her values, and her goals. She began to develop self-confidence and self-respect. The evolution from Superwoman to Boat Rocker had begun.

And more women like Emma will gradually realize that their potential lies beyond mastering technical knowledge. More and more women are looking to their work and profession as a part of their lifetime fulfillment, and in doing so, they are acquiring the tools necessary to advance professionally as well as personally.

Acquiring training in management is available in business schools and executive training institutes. Women who are trained in another profession can easily get excellent programs in decision-making, finance, management strategy, management style, conflict resolution, and organizational systems. Most of the Boat Rockers have had some or all of these courses, and in addition, have learned about power and how to feel comfortable with it and use it.

Armed with self-confidence as well as technical and interpersonal skills, Boat Rockers deviate from normal professional tracks and seek out leadership roles. Both Emma and Mary have positions of leadership and power, they are comfortable with their success and responsibilities, and they have the ability and willingness to share and help other women in their careers. Both use networks and support systems with other women in similar situations; both choose relationships which foster growth; both have left secure positions to try the unknown; both have been risk takers in order to increase their chances to make a greater impact on the world; both have absorbed a great deal of negative feedback from people who are insecure or jealous.

Boat Rockers are not only successful professionally. They are also generally happier in their personal lives. Their relationships with others are honest and sincere. They are aware of their limitations and do not hesitate to admit their weaknesses or to laugh at their mistakes.

Generally speaking, Boat Rockers have arrived at this stage by consciously working at developing themselves psychologically and emotionally. By trial and error, and even with the inevitable pain and setbacks they have experienced in trying to bring about changes and and in challenging the establishment, these women have not been deterred in acquiring the coping skills and self-esteem to match their professional proficiency and to attain their objectives. They rarely have goals or dreams they cannot achieve.

Boat Rockers can be summarized as women who can and will make major contributions to the world. They have the legitimate power to effect change. They have the courage to embrace success and defeats without flinching, and they have the generosity of spirit to help other aspiring women.

This discussion of Boat Rockers cannot be complete without mentioning the group of pseudo Boat Rockers. These are phonies. These women hold positions of power, and many are risk takers. They convey confidence and savvy with the appropriate worldly manner to convince large numbers of people that they are in fact competent leaders. But unlike the Boat Rockers, these imposters do not possess true self-esteem. They are not fully confident about their abilities or themselves. Many have managerial positions as a result of their gender, not their skills.

As the token female manager to whom the organization can point to show how progressive it is, these women are usually in over their heads. As a result, they are quite defensive and insecure and try to hide behind the cloak of feminism. In fact, they are far from being true feminists. They profess to advocate equal rights and opportunities for all women, but these are just hollow words. These women who got their positions because they are women are the very ones who will not lift one finger to help competent, talented women. These fakers are commonly referred to as "Queen Bees," "Black Widow Spiders," and "Women Crushers."

In my study and interviews with women all across the county, many middle managers kept referring to women as being their own worst enemies because those at the top are so jealous of any competition that they will cut off the proficient ones at the first opportunity. As one summed it up, "The saddest part of the entire situation is that, except for my family, the only ones who have helped me this far are men. If it had been left to women, there would be only male managers. Women are their own worst enemies."

A national coalition composed of six organizations working toward a mutual goal of placing more women in leadership positions provides a case study of the Queen Bee in action.

Each organization's leader had a long history of involvement with women's issues and an equally deep commitment to helping women acquire leadership skills and positions. Each of the six had impeccable credentials in education, training, and experience. Each had achieved success in her profession and the respect of her colleagues. Each understood the problems of women and had all the knowledge and coping skills to deal with them effectively.

With these strong backgrounds and minds, it seemed a foregone conclusion that the coalition would combine the talents and dedication of these top-notch women and would effect change exponentially.

What happened, instead, were sophisticated power plays and undermining strategies which led to the eventual demise of the coalition and its goals. Except for one or two, these women did not have enough self-confidence to share their thoughts, their resources, their successes with the others. There were backbiting, grandstanding, and great deal of feigned cooperation and support.

At the end of the second year, each was asked to submit, anonymously, comments and an evaluation of the coalitions. Some of the remarks about working together include:

1. We don't share openly with one another, although I have doubts it is possible.
2. We share our accomplishments, but it takes the form of "my dog is bigger than yours."
3. We are competitive
4. We know little about each others' personal lives, but we know more because of our coordinator.
5. We don't use good group process skills; we interrupt.
6. We operate solo.
7. We don't trust each other because of our different personalities.
8. If I really opened up, I don't think others could tolerate my candor or directness.
9. We've got our backs up over each others' style.
10. It is a forced network; we can't or won't use or rely on each others' strengths.

11. We know each others' project only superficially.
12. I don't need the other projects. I have my own network.
13. Some of us are alienated from the group.
14. We are six prima donnas in a room with one mirror.
15. We are polite in our dealings and dance around the real issues between us.

These comments coming from these women leaders pinpoint the difficulty women have in overcoming their traditional emotional and psychological upbringing. In principle there is no doubt that these women have applied their best talents and energies to helping other women. In reality it is much more difficult to work with others who are at the same level of accomplishment than it is to help those who obviously will never be a threat.

The lack of true self-esteem and a sense of worth does make women—and men—feel threatened when they know others know as much as they do. The immediate reaction is an emotional one rather than a cognitive one. Defense mechanisms are activated and barriers are set up. From then on, all efforts to communicate, cooperate, and succeed are blocked.

Just how prevalent are those Queen Bees? Probably more common than any woman would care to admit. And—truthfully—this behavior fuels the narrow-minded attitude that women don't have what it takes to be top leaders.

Interviews for this book uncovered Queen Bees at all levels, not just at the top. Whether they are first-line managers or state cabinet officers, all the Queen Bees showed task-specific self-esteem at best. All enjoy the limelight of being an upwardly mobile woman who hads broken through the barriers of male management. Most pay lip service to helping other women achieve their professional goals, but in reality they want to maintain their exclusivity. They don't really want the mass of women to have the same opportunities or advantages.

What these Queen Bees do not realize is that many of them were selected as token executives because they are not competent enough to threaten the real power structure. On those occasions when the value and quality of their work are questioned, Queen Bees take up a militant feminist stance. They become combative and accuse their superiors of once again showing favoritism to the old boy network and bias against women and their efforts. Using an aggressive smokescreen of feminism to sidetrack their critics, Queen Bees limit their professional growth. They are too busy playing the role of the defender of feminism to listen to performance evaluations that would help improve them.

In addition to stifling their own potential through their closed minds and closed communication styles, Queen Bees also make it harder for non-Queen Bees to overcome the negative female image they, the Queen Bees, have created. Top management often dismisses Queen Bee's lack of sold technical and management abilities as inherent female inadequacies.

Unlike male workers who usually rise and fall professionally based on their own personal merits, women are still often judged collectively rather than individually. And the modus operandi of Queen Bees adds much to counteract and severely damage the earnest efforts of Superwoman, Beyond Superwoman, and Boat Rockers, who are, in fact, vital, relevant professionals.

I believe that Queen Bees represent an aberration rather than a mainstream psychological stage. Just as there are aggressive, obnoxious men, there are Queen Bees. Just as there are obsequious men who will do whatever it takes to butter up the boss, there are Queen Bees.

While all of us have probably met and worked with Queen Bees and felt the sting of their ruthlessness, I feel that their psychological insecurities will eventually cause them to self destruct at some point in their careers. They do not have the most important personal characteristic of real Boat Rockers—comfort and honesty with themselves.

Boat Rockers have confidence and respect for themselves and others. Queen Bees are aggressive, self-absorbed, and suspicious. Boat Rockers are willing to share their knwledge and networks with other women. Queen Bees are so egocentric and possessive of their turf, they will undercut talented, promising women whenever they have a chance to do so. Boat Rockers use their experience and skills to work toward their goals. Queen Bees are so intent on self aggrandizement and status, they let the organization dictate their future.

It is important to know that Queen Bees exist and to acknowledge the lasting damage they can inflict on other women; however, I believe that they will eventually be replaced by Boat Rockers. Boat Rockers will succeed because they will demonstrate their commitment to and talent in achieving high levels of success using cooperation rather than confrontation, their clarity of purpose and their ability to respond to criticism and adversitites with objectivity and innovative solutions. They will not work to restrain social traditions as Queen Bee does, but will work to expand them. Boat Rockers will preserve instead the best motives and resilient spirit of being human.

Stage V:
The Grand Prix Winner

Finally we come to a level of psychological development that so far has been achieved by only a handful of women. As the name implies, Grand Prix Winners are movers and shakers who have convincingly and effectively translated their thoughts and visions into a sustained and valuable influence on evolutionary—if not sometimes revolutionary—changes in many economic, educational, political, and social systems and structures.

Armed with their personal dreams and visions of improving existing systems and opportunities, these women have used their skills, inventiveness, and their uncompromisingly firm commitment to their values to interact with, as well as challenge, the deeply entrenched systems.

These women, through their efforts, have made an impact on correcting many unconscionable social and economic conditions. And while individually they may not have changed dramatically the course of history, collectively they have steadily altered the direction and emphases of our society.

In an environment where preservation of the status quo provides financial, political, and social success and power to those who consent and agree with prevailing goals and modus operandi, reformists with no more than a pure heart and a just cause will find the full force of the establishment used against them to quiet and stifle them as quickly and as permanently as possible. So it takes more than a well meaning idealist to effect large-scale changes. It takes a realist who understands the stakes, the obstacles, the game-playing, and the art of cooperation and compromise. Grand Prix Winners are those realist. Drawing on their past, experiences, successes and failures, and using their and keen perspicacity, Grand Prix Winners have become top-level competitors and top-level winners.

In addition to their successes acknowledged by the world in the professional arena, Grand Prix Winners have also worked at and succeeded in being well-rounded human beings. They have not singlemindedly pursued their careers to the exclusion of either themselves as women or the other people who are part of their lives. They have consciously charted their professional and private lives that will broaden and fulfill them in dimensions which demand good judgment, dedication, and down-to-earth humanness.

These street smart and generous-spirited women are rare. Although there are millions of American women who have as much talent and potential as the Grand Prix Winners, the overwhelming majority do not feel that the goal is worth the extraordinary effort and the personal sacrifices they would have to make, so they stop short, fully satisfied with their accomplishments as Beyond Superwomen and Boat Rockers. For most women, it is too difficult emotionally and psychologically to constantly defy convention in order to change themselves and society. The stresses induced by pioneering new challenges to the existing systems and by standing alone when necessary seem to be borne only by those extraordinary women—and men—who are willing to pay that price in their quest to make a difference in the world.

This chapter discusses the paths these women have taken to arrive at this level of psychological development, the obstacles and dilemmas they encountered, and the methods they used to overcome them. This chapter also deals with key questions about Grand Prix Winners: How do they do it? What kind of magical combinations have they put together? What kind of people are they? How tough and ruthless are they to set their course and calculatingly fulfill their goals?

As in the entire process of psychological development of women, the Grand Prix Winners arrived at this stage gradually and imperceptibly. There were no sudden revelations or dramatic ascensions to power and success. Rather, Grand Prix Winners are those exceptional women who consciously and decisively sought both personal development and professional challenges throughout their lives. They worked their way through each stage: Superwoman, Beyond Superwoman, and Boat Rocker. With each successive stage, the Grand Prix Winner gained insights and skills from her experiences and self-assessments. Along the way, the Grand Prix Winner also gradually developed a firm sense of who she is, what her strengths and weaknesses are, what her accomplishments have been and are likely to be, and how she can use her position and talents to change and improve the existing system.

The previous chapters have dealt with some of the major components of development, such as awareness of the problem, assertiveness, self-esteem, power, clear goals, and training. Beyond Superwoman and Boat Rockers have some of these traits and continue to make progress through a high level of awareness and a determination to be better self-actualized. Most of the Beyond Superwomen and Boat Rockers are quite satisfied with their level of development and professional success. But those Beyond Superwomen and Boat Rockers, who finally emerge as Grand Prix Winners, have worked very hard at acquiring as many professional and interpersonal skills as they could and have maximized their options and opportunities.

Grand Prix Winners have resolved most of the inner conflicts between traditional values and feminist independence and between conventional behavior and self-actualization. They have integrated their interests, experiences, and values after years of struggle. And they have risen to positions of influence and power at the same time they have been developing confidence in themselves and their abilities.

Unlike the women in other stages of development, Grand Prix Winners have overcome the compassion and nurturing trap we discussed earlier. They don't feel the compulsion to be the "earth mother" and to provide warmth, sympathy, and help to everyone who wants it. They don't have Superwoman's need to be loved by everyone and to be a friend to everybody.

Grand Prix Winners have lived through those stages and have systematically worked through the inner conflicts and external social pressures to conform to conventional expectations. They have forged their own paths to professional success and personal fulfillment.

They have been able to straddle successfully both worlds by walking that thin line between mainstream establishment and their own intellectual and psychological independence. In doing so, they developed reputations as team players and as intelligent and reliable women who have the ability to make hard and important decisions, to be fair and objective, and to be excellent leaders. As a result, Grand Prix Winners gained and hold power. They can and do influence the outcome of private- and public-sector decisions, influence public opinion, and effect the gradual change of social systems and social values. Grand Prix Winners are exactly where they have always wanted to be—on the front lines working as movers and shakers to change the world.

Grand Prix Winners, like Boat Rockers, do not leave their professional and personal fate to luck. They set goals and plan their careers early and worked constantly to expand their options. They have made every effort to influence luck. Earlier chapters addressed the severe limitations that Hearth Tenders, Superwomen, and some Beyond Superwomen impose on themselves by unquestioningly adopting conventional values and behavior. As Ruth Holcomb pointed out in her book *Women Making It*, these women merely cope and reach out of dreams that will never come true because they don't plan.[1] As a result, their outlook and opportunities are determined more by their socialization than by their ambition or skills. Grand Prix Winners, on the other hand, systematically worked to overcome the traditions to which many women are chronically prone and in so doing, they took charge of their own lives.

Grand Prix Winners have had clear goals and sought supplemental education in their profession and in psychological adaptation and coping. They know what they want to accomplish and the positions they must hold in order to achieve their goals. They have worked hard to get this point: they set priorities in their professional and personal lives. They know that they don't have the energy or time to do everything for everybody—as Hearth Tender and Superwomen try to do. Grand Prix Winners became assertive and overcame the traditions of being all things to all people. They became confident enough to accept their limitations and mistakes without feeling jeopardized and threatened. They have developed effective interpersonal and management skills so that they can delegate tasks, resolve conflicts, and manage themselves and others without feeling guilty as Superwoman does.

Grand Prix Winners are risk takers. But they carefully select the time and circumstances. They do not ever jeopardize their entire career or financial security. Unlike many women who remain loyal to their philosophical ideals throughout their lives and make decisions based on those ideals, Grand Prix Winners—and some Beyond Superwomen and Boat Rockers—weigh the odds of winning before they make decisions. The have arrived where they are because they have made decisions and persuaded others that their goals are worthwhile, and through their successes and increased challenges and responsibilities, they have ascended into positions of power.

Grand Prix Winners, unlike most women, almost always land on their feet after losing. They never take defeat personally, as Hearth Tender, Superwomen and some Beyond Superwomen do. They never feel that a defeat is a sign of being incompetent or unworthy. They assess the results, come face to face with their limitations, and then start looking for new opportunities. This objectivity and unwavering faith in their own abilities are the primary strengths that separate Grand Prix Winners from women in other stages of psychological development.

Grand Prix Winners feel comfortable with themselves as people so that they are willing to help others, especially other women. Unlike the Queen Bees discussed earlier, the Grand Prix Winner is genuinely supportive of the successes of other women and actively works to help other women by providing professional opportunities, interpersonal counseling, encouragement, or by becoming a mentor. Grand Prix Winners feel that the traditions that have stifled women and created enormous psychological conflicts for them can be overcome gradually through role models and support systems.

Professionally, Grand Prix Winners are not bewildered by the unfathomable mazes of power plays and organizational dynamics. Rather, they have learned the ins and outs of these systems and apply their strengths and skills incisively as well as imaginatively in both organizational and power structures.

They have overcome obstacles that are anchored in convenience, in tradition, in fear, and in social pressures and expectations. Their persistence and indomitable independence ultimately result in their personal successes, which provide role models for other women.

Grand Prix Winners are powerful women. They are in positions where the control money, resources, and information. And with this control, they can determine directions and decisions that affect millions of Americans. Unlike women in other stages, Grand Prix Winners do not approach power with fear and trembling. They do not fear success like Superwomen. They are not content with the success and power they have achieved like Beyond Superwomen and some Boat Rockers. Rather, Grand Prix Winners seek greater challenges and bigger responsibilities constantly.

These women do not view power as a burden that jeopardizes their personal relationships as Superwomen do. They are not satisfied with accomplishments and successes they know represent only a part of their potential and capabilities.

From the time they were teenagers, most Grand Prix Winners have had grand visions. That constant vision has influenced their education, decisions, and determination to acquire the skills and experience necessary to effect that vision.

Grand Prix Winners do not face life as passive women who are swept through and around time by nostalgic traditions. Rather they are activists who reach up and out as insistent and passionate players who seek to inform and transform the world.

Although this short description may make them sound bigger than life, Grand Prix Winners are truly high achievers who have worked very hard to get to the top. Their determination and goals have set them apart from other women.

The following is a summary of those characteristics that distinguish Grand Prix Winners from women in other stages of psychological development. They have:

1. Overcome limitations and stereotypes imposed by society.
2. Developed and acquired the major components of leadership.
3. Gained power.

Overcome limitations and stereotypes. As we discussed in previous chapters, the stereotyped roles for women include those of the mother, the sex symbol, the office pet. These roles are designed to keep women limited to positions and places where they will not be a competitive threat and where their sexuality is defined in traditional ways. As a consequence very few women are found in leadership positions even today.

For those women who chose careers, they still operated under two great limitations. According to Hennig and Jardim's study of 45 women managers, women generally have ill-defined perceptions about their attitudes toward these careers. They are also fairly unaware of the organizational environment in which they work.[2]

The women in the Hennig and Jardim study viewed their careers as an opportunity for personal growth, self-fulfillment, and making a contribution to their employer and society. They did not feel the need for recognition or rewards as part of their career definition. Making career decisions rather late, after they had been in the job for 10 years, these women were generally passive and did not build on their past experiences and successes. They accepted assignments as they were given and did not seek positions which would increase their levels of expertise and career progress.

Rosabeth Moss Kanter also verified these traits in her research. She found that women tended to become isolated and invisible in an organization. Sometimes, as a lone woman in a male group, a woman would reinforce her own isolation by a series of accommodative strategies by keeping a low profile and by not taking credit for her own accomplishments.[3]

Men, on the other hand, view careers as a series of jobs and a path leading upward toward recognition and reward. From an early age, men have expected to work to support at least themselves. Only a small percentage of women come face to face with this issue in their younger years.[4]

Women have always thought that they can get ahead in their careers by the sheer strength and depth of their knowledge and by their conscientiousness. They are convinced that self-improvement programs will bolster their success on their career ladder and have also been inordinately dependent on the formal structure of organizations for their professional recognition and promotions. But they either do not understand or underestimate the importance of the informal system of relationships. They seem to be unaware that informal networks provide information sharing, loyalty, mutual benefit, support, and protection.

To be sure, structural components of an organization are vital to a woman's career advancement and behavior. But in organizations as well as in their personal lives, women are usually stereotyped as nurturing supportive followers while men stereotyped are as powerful and influential leaders.

Not only are men and women perceived to be different from each other, but society also expects their behavior to fall into gender specific stereotypes. And for the most part, they do; their actions, responses, and attitudes are fairly predictable.

But sometimes men and women change their styles of behavior noticeably. Elizabeth Aries found that men and women in mixed groups often altered both their attitude and behavior. For example, Aries discovered that men in mixed groups tend to be less competitive than they are in all-male groups. They also show a greater interest and orientation toward people when women are in the group.

In mixed groups men tend to express their feelings and make references to themselves more than in all-male groups. They talk less about sports and amusements. In other words, men seem to develop a more personal orientation and a decreased aggressive competitive behavior when they are in mixed groups.

Women, on the other hand, decreased their interaction with other women when men were in the group; they also talked less about their homes and family. Aries feels that women may want to present themselves as more competent and independent when males are present, but they temper this professional behavior by being more passive and talking less than they do in all-female groups. When men are in a group, women initiate only 34% of the total interaction.[5]

Women also show a greater tentativeness and uncertainty about their views and opinions when they are in a mixed group. In fact, women showed an extraordinarily high level of agreement with men's beliefs when they were in the presence of men.

Aries concluded that the low level of interaction between women in mixed groups can be traced back to women's traditional competition with each other for the attention and affection of men. It can also be traced to women's low regard for women and high regard for men and what men do.

The conclusion about mixed groups is that they seem to benefit men more than women. Men show more variations in their interpersonal style, and women become more restricted.

The stereotypes by society and the limitations imposed by women on themselves have had devastating effects on the psychological and emotional growth of women even in the age of liberation. These barriers have kept intelligent and talented women from reaching their full potential.

In her book *Our Inner Conflicts* psychiatrist Karen Horney describes the personality traits which limit growth. She asserts that a person who lives with unresolved conflicts wastes an enormous amount of energy because she is basically divided and can never put all of her energy into any one thing. She always wants to pursue two or more incompatible goals—as Superwoman does. Even when a person with conflicts tries to demonstrate singlemindedness of purpose, Horney says, it is out of desperation rather than integration.[6]

The inner conflicts result in three behaviors: indecisiveness, ineffectualness, and inertia. These three prominent characteristics describe Superwoman to a tee. Superwoman's indecision and procrastination stem from her need to be accepted and liked by everyone. Her ineffectualness results from being a "behind-the-scenes" helper. She never takes proper credit for new ideas or success because she feels it would alienate her from her co-workers and friends. And her inertia is a form of paralysis of action and initiative. She prefers to react and respond rather than to initiate.

Hearth Tender is not aware of conflicts or limitations, so she continues to function within the milieu of her own world of tradition and expectation. Some Beyond Superwomen and Boat Rockers are working to overcome these obstacles. And Grand Prix Winners have overcome the barriers and stereotype roles all women face. But the stifling outcomes of these limitations and behaviors are fully embodied in Superwoman.

Dot is a perfect example of a Grand Prix Winner. Born in West Virginia as the third of four children, Dot became a reporter after college. "During the '60s I wanted to be a reporter in the South and to cover civil rights and politics. I applied to become a general assignment reporter, but my first job was fashion editor. I didn't want to get slotted into women's issues, so I created topics to cover and set my own agenda. I did feature articles which allowed me a great deal of freedom.

"My goals in life were to get an education, to graduate from college, to get married, to have children, and to stay with them until I was thirty-five or forty. My mother was my role model, and she was a homemaker. She had worked on a doctorate but dropped out to have children. There was no questions that I would do the same."

Despite her traditional views, Dot actually had to overcome fewer inner conflicts than most women. With parents who encouraged their children to be socially responsible, to achieve, and to make an impact on society, Dot developed a sense of beliefs early in life. Her mother, by example, conveyed a value and goal system.

"I never moved progressively through the ranks of the newspaper hierarchy. I did not become an assistant editor, associate editor, or editor. I made a choice to stay in news. The ranks in newspapers are quite clearly defined, and there are fewer power games than in other corporations. And reporters by their very nature are independent thinkers. I know that I certainly was. I never had any difficulties with the concepts of right and wrong. I was always strong-willed and opinionated."

Today, Dot at 47 has completed her training program to become a newspaper publisher for the Knight Ridder chain. She was tapped four years ago as she finished her second term as national president of the League of Women Voters.

The president of Knight Ridder had known Dot since the two were reporters on the same newspaper 20 years ago. He had followed her career as a journalist, as the editor and part owner of a business newspaper, and as the president of LWV. And when Knight Ridder decided to recruit women actively to manage and publish some of its newspapers, Dot was a logical choice.

Both her parents were well educated and took active roles in instilling strong value systems in the four children. Each child was schooled in the importance of a good education and the Protestant ethic of hard work.

"I remember that we talked a lot about things going on in the world," Dot relates. "We talked about the differences between right and wrong. As a result, all of us ended up selecting professions which allow us to have an impact on policies and laws. My older sister is an editor. My second sister is the owner of a business, and my brother is in the West Virginia legislature. You could say that the influence was very strong."

While at her first newspaper Dot married a fellow reporter, and they moved to Kentucky. Also from a family of high achievers, Dot's husband Don went to law school at night while he was urban affairs editor for the Louisville newspaper. Dot stayed home with their two children and did volunteer work for nonprofit organizations.

When Dot returned to journalism, she became an editor of a business newspaper of which she was part owner. She continued with the editorship after she was elected national president of the League of Women Voters. But it became too taxing, so she sold the paper.

The League of Women Voters' presidency was a great opportunity for Dot. "I had an opportunity to deal with important national issues, meet with national and world leaders, make decisions for the league membership, and serve as spokesman for the group. The confidence I had was bolstered by the experiences, but I think my background as a reporter gave me the ability to deal with leaders comfortably and easily.

"I felt comfortable with both the responsibilities and the power."

And now as she assumes the top position of one of the Knight Ridder papers, she once more conveys her commitment to social responsibility and her ability to handle power. "I feel comfortable with success. I look forward to using my position on the newspaper to achieve things. I would like to push the public toward progressivity and to champion causes. The newspaper as a community leader needs to help a community achieve what it wants and needs." Although she grew up with conventional values and goals, Dot developed beyond the unwritten confines and stereotypes of society and continued to grow professionally and personally even during those years when she was raising children and doing volunteer work. Her sense of social responsibility, coupled with a confidence in her abilities, allowed her to seek out positions far beyond the dreams of other traditional women. There is no doubt that Dot will use her power and influence to mold social attitudes and values and to effect beneficial changes in the area her newspaper serves.

Dot typifies Grand Prix Winners by constantly seeking new challenges to stretch herself.

Have components of leadership. Many women have become experts in their professions; many have gained recognition for their achievements. But very few are making it to the top. They seem to lack those special skills and traits which would make it possible to get to the seats of power and leadership.

Grand Prix Winners are those few who have what it takes to get to the top. It is a combination of their family upbringing and their acquired skills. First of all, they were not raised by their families to be passive princesses who waited for a prince to rescue them. Rather, their backgrounds show that their parents instilled strong values and encouraged them to aim high. As a result, they grew up with ambitions and values that were untraditional enough to let them develop great psychological and emotional strength. With that security they struck out on their own in directions few women had charted. Second, these women also set their goals early and prepared themselves for successive challenges. Third, they are risk takers who are willing to take unpopular positions and to defend those positions. Fourth, with strong family support and encouragement they developed good self-esteem. They are not hampered by neuroses or depression and take full responsibility for their actions and decisions. Fifth, they have developed very good interpersonal skills and management styles. They are accessible to everyone and have an easygoing style which makes people comfortable about working with them. They are objective and listen to the views of others. Sixth, they have set up good networks with colleagues and other women. They have learned that information and access and mutual help come more often from informal networks than through the formal organizational structure.

As Karen Horney and Ruth Holcomb have stated in their works, it takes a great deal of effort and a positive conflict-free state of mind and a strong, independent nature for a woman to get her career off the ground. Until recently, women weren't driven to excel professionally. Many were professionals, but they always viewed their first responsibilities as their families. And even in two-income families, it was the mother's responsibility to hire the housekeeper, find the baby-sitter, and take care of the special family events such as birthdays and attending school events. Consequently, many women selected professions which were less prestigious and often became nurses, teachers, or social workers. And even in those professions they rarely reached the top.

Women who grew up in traditional settings were not any less intelligent than today's woman. They also had ambitions, aspirations, and dreams, but they were overwhelmed by the traditions and myths of the society in which the grew up. For those rare women who forged careers and set their own independent course before the women's movement of the 1960s, it required both perseverance and a strong will to combat public disapproval. Since the 1960s the social and individual changes have made possible more individual growth and have opened up opportunities and minds. Women now live in a more receptive society and are helped by a network of women and supportive men who encourage them to fulfill themselves.

Hennig and Jardim found that women must make some fundamental changes in their professional skills as they move from supervision to management. In their book *The Managerial Woman*, they outline their findings as goal setting, problem-solving, learning systems, and formal systems of relationships, team sports, and risk-taking. In their study of 25 women who made it to the top, Hennig and Jardim profiled a composite of these women. Most of them used their technical skills and competence during the first 10 years of their careers. They were able to use their professional abilities as a means of controlling interpersonal relationships. By the time they were in their late 30s, they had moved up to positions in higher levels of middle management. They made these changes from middle to upper management because they elected to acquire new personal and organizational skills. They all rose to president or vice president of their firms.

These 25 superachievers had planned their careers and sustained their pace and commitment to their professions. They built on their achievements. They did not feel encumbered by their genders or their cultural values and sought recognition in their chosen fields. They acquired all those skills and traits that society had told generations of women were unbecoming and unfeminine: assertiveness, high intelligence, competitiveness, ambition. They made choices and decisions which were considered exclusively male prerogatives. They made their career choices based on their talents, training, and interests. They did not base their choices on society's view of proper female professions.[7]

Traditional values. The 25 women who formed the core of Hennig and Jardim's book *The Managerial Woman* all came from families that debunked the prevalent and popular attitude about female inferiority. Their fathers all encouraged them to be achievers, and while other adolescent girls were trying to be popular with the boys, these women strengthened and clarified their concepts of themselves during those teenage years.

Joanne, 54, grew up in a family which set the stage for her future success. She inherited the leftwing labor activism in which her Roman Catholic Irish family had been involved for generations in Pennsylvania. Her father, a policeman, made sure his three daughters acquired the family's commitment to fairness and justice, and Joanne's grandmother taught her the nuts and bolts of grassroots political action.

"From our family tradition of blue collar coal miners, I was exposed to the labor movement and hard-core politics from the time I was a small child. My parents and grandmother never preached about value systems; they demonstrated it through their involvement in movements and activities that promoted equality of treatment and opportunity.

"My grandmother always told me that every American has something to offer this country, but in order to have an opportunity, you have to have control. And my parents reinforced that idea by telling me that I should aim to make the world better."

As heirs to their family's strong social conscience and achievements, Joanne and her two sisters, like the twenty-five women in the Hennig and Jardim study, were encouraged to participate in activities which are not specifically female oriented. For example, Joannes's father persuaded her to learn judo. This martial art taught Joanne not only self-defense but also helped her develop confidence in her physical abilities. She also played football when most teenage girls were worried about fashions, dates, and physical appeal.

"I learned about physical competence and the meaning of playing on a team. And my parents thought this skill was great. "My dad also pushed my sisters and me into speech and debating.

"Not being raised traditionally helped me a lot. It built my confidence and allowed me to become independent at a time when the conventional woman was raised to be dependent.

"The open attitude and environment at home when I was a child helped me develop a better sense of who I am. And I have always taken responsibility for my own decisions and my own life."

Joanne was the first generation of her family to go to college. She attended a private woman's college for her undergraduate work. "My father strongly advocated womens' colleges and told me that I would get practice in being a leader at a woman's college.

"I really wanted to be a lawyer, but there were no scholarships at the time. My family couldn't afford to pay the tuition, so I went to graduate school in psychology with a scholarship.

"Psychology allowed me to work with people but not to change systems."

Joanne practiced as a clinical psychologist until she started her family. Like Dot she did not work while her five children were growing up, but she did volunteer work.

"I volunteered with the local League of Women Voters and worked on model cities and public housing issues. I helped put together a public interest law firm. I lobbied for the LWV on Capitol Hill for eight years on environmental and strip mining issues. I was living in York, Pennsylvania, and later in Massachusetts, and I spent at least one week a month in Washington. "Lobbying gave me a chance to work for change. That is what I always wanted."

Through her networks and experience Joanne rose to her current position of president of women and Foundations/Corporate Philanthropy in New York. She yields enormous influence.

"We encourage foundations to fund more projects that deal with women and girls, and we also try to increase the number of professional women on foundation staffs. Our organization serves as a source of new ideas for grants and as an education resource for grant makers. By highlighting specific women's issues, we hope that we can expand the horizons and commitments by foundations.

"I love this job. It brings together so many things I've done—social policy research, politics, networking—and what I was raised to believe in—social justice."

Grand Prix Winners unknowingly were being prepared for later success and achievements through the upbringing, values, and unqualified support of their parents. From childhood on they were less encumbered by conventional female behavior and norms. They developed a set of goals, ambitions, and a higher level of self-confidence which separated them from the average American woman. And armed with these assets Grand Prix Winners have been able to leapfrog over many of the psychological and emotional barriers which hinder the growth of so many American women.

Clear goals. In some aspects, Dot, Joanne, and many other Grand Prix Winners grew up no differently from other women. They were taught that women devote themselves to being mothers and homemakers, even though they are well-educated and have worked professionally. Dot's mother discontinued her work on her Ph.D. to have children. Joanne's mother worked for 15 years as a bookkeeper before her three daughters were born. And although both women elected to follow their mothers and dropped out of their professions while their own children were young, Grand Prix Winners like Dot and Joanne never wavered in their ultimate goals of being able to influence social opinion and social systems.

However, the timetables and execution of Grand Prix Winners' clear goals are quite different from those of men. As we have already pointed out, men are much more deliberate about their career paths and career decisions. Each new position is part of a growth sequence which prepares them for the next.

Grand Prix Winners, like Boat Rockers, have clear goals, but their career paths and interruptions reflect their adaptability to the dual role of career woman-mother as well as the importance of their families. Although they never lost sight of their career goals, Grand Prix Winners—and some Boat Rockers—placed them at varying levels of priority during different stages of their lives. And even through those years when being at home with the children took precedence over their careers, Grand Prix winners were actively involved in projects and organizations that kept them intellectually up-to-date and provided them with skills and training they could use when they reentered their professions later. In a directed but flexible way they were planning and preparing for the future.

During the course of their volunteer activities both Dot and Joanne received formal leadership training in group dynamics, assertiveness, time and stress management and management techniques. In addition, the volunteer arena developed their abilities to work with others as well as to lead them.

The Grand Prix Winners who followed a continuous career path used their technical skills and competence as a way of controlling interpersonal relationships and achieving early success. As they moved to higher levels of middle management they acquired additional skills to do the job. Those skills are identical with the ones Dot and Joanne developed in their volunteer work.

These women also sought out successive challenges. As president of the League of Women Voters Dot served as its national spokesman, met 20 heads of state, and moderated a nationally televised debate between two U.S. presidential candidates. Joanne helped organize a public interest law firm, lobbied on Capitol Hill, and conducted public policy research on welfare and public housing.

It is clear that goal setting, planning, and leadership training and experience were instrumental in preparing Grand Prix Winners to ultimately reach the top.

Joanne's summary speaks for many Grand Prix Winners: "I built management skills by doing it. Through experience in management and budgeting, you develop a good sense of leading an organization.

"Many men and women are timid about making big management decisions. To be in charge means bearing the responsibility and making those decisions. If you make a mistake, there will always be a self-correcting process. The world will not go up in flames."

Risk Takers. The term *risk taker* may conjure up the image of a wildly adventurous daredevil who will defy all odds in breathtaking feats. And while many of us have had thoughts about throwing caution to the winds, we almost always choose reality over fantasy.

Grand Prix Winners are realists and dreamers at the same time. They combine an idealist's vision of a better world with a pragmatic recognition of the pace and ways reforms and progress can be made. Their interpretations of systems and organizations are far from oversimplified or reductionist interpretations. Rather, they show a sophisticated, realistic, cognitive maturity. They show strength and a value system which were conceived and nurtured in their early lives and developed through many layers of understanding as they progress through their careers and lives.

These women did not careen through life from one misguided notion to another. Instead, they used their acquired experience and achievements and their sharp analytical faculties to determine when and how to take risks.

The risks Grand Prix Winners take are the same risks that high-achieving men take. They are willing to take unpopular or new stands on issues and to defend them. Far from being defiant nonconformists, Grand Prix Winners stake out those risks in arenas when they feel it is both necessary and feasible to do so.

Risk taking is probably the single most important trait that separates Grand Prix Winners from other women. They are able and willing to take the heat when necessary.

As Karen Horney pointed out in *Our Inner Conflicts*, most women are not willing to assume responsibility for their decisions or their own lives. If something goes wrong, they blame others for it. They have so many psychological and emotional conflicts, they have developed a helplessness and fear that prevents them from standing on their own.[8]

Decision making presupposes the capacity to take responsibility for its success or failure. The inherent risk lies in making the wrong choice and having to bear the consequences without blaming others.

Joanne and Dot are both risk takers in their positions and actions.

As Joanne said, "I never bought into somebody else's plan for my life. My father taught us early that we will assume more and more responsibility for our own lives. He also told me that I should grow up to be a leader. And with a family of political activists, it was clear that I was never raised to be nice or to be intimidated by anybody or anything."

Many women view risk as negative and alien to their nature. Since American women were generally raised in a traditional, nonconfrontive female environment, it is easy to see their point of view. As we saw in the Superwoman stage, many women turn down promotions because they don't want to risk being cut off from their friends and the familiarity of their jobs.

Hennig and Jardim underscored this trait by pointing out that "many middle managers make decisions on the basis of their own sense of security and legitimacy. This orientation is an inward preoccupation which blunts their ability to judge people and circumstances objectively. They see others in terms of the impact they have on their own sense of inadequacy."[9]

Superwomen are reluctant to ask questions or make decisions because they are afraid it might show ignorance or because the decision might be in error. Unknowingly they block their ability to learn and grow.

Their lack of self-confidence creates great anxiety levels and a constant need to prove themselves all the time—to themselves and to the men around them.

Grand Prix Winners, on the other hand, have an outward orientation. They focus on their long-range goals and how they are going to achieve them. They reach out for opportunities, new skills, and challenges without the high level of anxiety that plagues other women. The 25 superachievers whom Hennig and Jardim studied all risked social ostracism by rejecting sororities in college and marrying late in life. Instead, they pursued their careers; they have very few women friends and had very few long-term relationships with men outside work. None married until she was at least 35 years old, all married men at least 10 years older than they, and none had children.

Their biggest risk was rejecting their own gender heritage. They did not deal with this conflict until they were in their late 30s. By then they had risen to high enough levels in their careers that they no longer felt the need to consciously avoid the femininity of the traditional woman. It was now all right to reestablish old social contacts and a softer feminine image. They had already established themselves professionally and personally and had demonstrated that common female "weaknesses" and inferiority complex did not apply to them.

Neither Dot nor Joanne has ever had any difficulty expressing her own opinions or participating in activities which are socially controversial.

For example, Joanne worked for the establishment of a ward system of representation in Pennsylvania. "I learned from my grandmother that the designated-seat ward system was preferable to the "at-large" system. It enabled minorities to hold positions; it would help break down existing barriers and allow them to have a voice as well as access to power. Minorities—and this included blue-collar Irish Catholics—would never have been able to penetrate the "at-large" system."

When Joanne and her sisters each turned 16, their father made each promise never to join an organization that discriminates against people or races. With this strong family philosophy, Joanne plunged into the civil rights movement and participated as much as she could. She also was selected to debate Phyllis Schlafly about ERA.

"I am a radical feminist, but I was chosen to debate Ms. Schlafly because we have similar backgrounds. We are both Roman Catholics, came from working class parents, went to college on scholarships, and had large families.

"I never avoid confrontation, In fact, I like it. I like to mix up a situation and see who comes up on top.

"I never dump on a weaker person, but I will take on and dump on a peer at any time."

Wanda, 63, took the ultimate risk—one that jeopardized her career and professional future and took a massive toll on her personal life. She filed a class-action suit against her employer on the grounds of sex discrimination and persevered for 10 years, enduring circumstances so oppressive and severe, they made Ulysses's odyssey look like a leisurely vacation.

Wanda was a program director for a large corporation. During her 20 years with the company, she had become the only woman director of three program directors in the company. Her great technical competence and a good understanding of internal politics, combined with a keen mind and winning personality, resulted in Wanda's strong record of accomplishment and recognition. She thought her career with this company was set for life.

Wanda was savvy enough to know that she could stay at the top as long as she wanted—provided she abide by the game rules of the corporation. But her basic values would not allow her to turn her head when she saw corporate policies she felt were injustices to employees. The unequal employee treatment she saw the corporation practicing had bothered her for a long time, and she couldn't figure out the best way to right this situation. Finally, measure and form were given to her lifelong philosophy and values.

Men and women in this corporation were being treated differently. "Women with equal skills, education, and responsibilities were being paid less than their male counterparts. I started keeping notes on this practice, which was verified when I got a copy of the company's pay scales for men and women. Women's pay scales were way below those of comparable jobs held by men. "I brought this pay scale discrepancy to the attention of the new vice president who was in charge of my division."

He was immediately uncomfortable with her inquiry as well as with her abilities, knowledge about the division, and level of professional self-confidence.

"The vice president never discussed the sex discrepancy with me. Instead, he suggested that I might want to transfer to another position or take an early retirement. There is no doubt that he felt I was a potential troublemaker and wanted me out of the way as soon as possible."

Wanda had grown up on a farm in Michigan. Homesteading and a livelihood dictated by equal efforts from every family member helped create the egalitarianism among sexes unique in the United States since the frontier movement. Wanda's family was no exception.

"We grew up in a small rural community. Everybody knew everybody else; we were like a large extended family. The value system of an agricultural people provided life values which consisted of persistence, determination, commitment to the land. The general philosophy was to make the best of what you had."

Her parents had each gone through the tenth grade in school, but the lack of formal education did not seem to hinder their abilities to function well as farmers, human beings, and role models for their children.

"My parents had great respect for each other; there were no male-female stereotypes, and they treated my brother, my sister, and me equally. The middle child of three, Wanda "had no ego problem growing up because both my parents were so supportive. I though the world was going to be my oyster."

During World War II Wanda joined the Navy at the age of 19 and was trained as a radio and communications specialist. Following the war and a short-lived marriage, she enrolled at Michigan State. Armed with a bachelor's degree in textiles and clothing, she set out to teach. Marriage led instead to living in South America for four years and to working while her new husband completed his Ph.D. During the course of the traditional American marriage, family, and support for spouse, Wanda did not work in her trained field but acquired the experience and knowledge in management and administration which would take her to a very high level.

When the corporate vice president was unresponsive about the pay scale discrimination based on sex, Wanda filed a complaint with the Equal Employment Opportunities Commission and received the right to sue. She then filed a class-action suit on behalf of all the women in the corporation.

Knowing that this action would probably mean the end of her career with the corporation, Wanda decided to really test the policies of the corporation. She did not resign her job but continued to perform her duties as program director. The next eight years were a "living hell. There was one harassment after another. Top management and its lackeys plagued me about everything. I was constantly being reprimanded, interrogated for my 'behavior'—which was never really defined—for malfeasance, nonfeasance, for vacation time, for every detail of my program. In addition, the company must have threatened my staff; they were cajoled and manipulated into reporting my activities and anything else about me that the vice president wanted to know.

"My program operations and finances were examined by the company's auditing department; there were two management studies done at a cost to the company of $750,000 to determine my program's efficiency and efficacy. The private statisticians I hired at my own expense to interpret the studies indicated that either the management experts did not know what they were doing or produced studies to discredit me professionally.

"The sex discrimination suit was yet another nightmare. Little did I know that it was just the beginning. The corporation tried to wear me down because its attorneys figured that I could not last as long as they could. They had access to the best legal minds and much greater financial resources. Talk about David and Goliath! Even my own lawyers were intimidated.

"During the 10-year length of the case, I had four sets of lawyers, but the meaner the corporation got, the more determined I became. In the end I won. I was awarded 10 years' back pay, damages, and attorney's fees. If it weren't for the continued support of strong feminists, friends, and my team of lawyers, I might have thrown in the towel long ago.

"Standing up for the principle is great in the abstract. In reality, it tests your sanity, your pocketbook, courage you never knew you had, and your spirit. And when it was over, I had no family to share it with. My mother had had a stroke, my father had died and my only child had been killed.

"I'm glad I did it. I hope it will set a precedent for other sex discrimination cases, and I hope my action will make it better for women in the future. As for me, I'm picking up the pieces and trying to get on with my own life. It was on hold for a decade."

Wanda represents the ultimate risk taker. She undertook a suit for all women and won for all women. The personal price she paid was more than most women—or men—would be willing to pay. It was courageous and selfless against what seemed like insurmountable odds, in a system where justice often is not done. And quite probably, if the case had gone to trial, Wanda would have found out that in reality all people are not equal in the eyes of the law. Those who win have the deepest resources for legal representation. But it was Wanda's constant determination and unwavering purpose that won in the end. This courage and ability to take big risks most clearly distinguish Grand Prix Winners from others and provide them with greater opportunities to convert their imagination and indignation into substantive changes to existing values and systems.

Good self esteem. In her book *Our Inner Conflict* Karen Horney discusses the compulsive neurotic behavior which drives so many women to seek safety rather than self-actualization. They have conflicts between what they want to do and what they actually do. And most women tend to fulfill the role of Superwoman because society expects it. While there is a satisfaction in assuming these roles and being a helper and friend to everyone who asks, these women also feel isolated, helpless, afraid, and depressed.[10]

Horney points out further that conflicts are normal. During the course of life each person—male and female—asks himself to examine, appraise, and resolve his personal conflicts between values and ambitions, integrity and self interests, social traditions and independence. Many people, like Grand Prix Winners, have consciously made the effort to resolve these conflicts so that they re-emerge with a stronger sense of values and purpose. As a result, they are decisive, confident, and willing to assume full responsibility for their lives and actions. Those like Superwoman, on the other hand, who are afraid to acknowledge or deal with their conflicts never clarify their values and remain trapped in a psychological prison they built around themselves. They are never able to determine their own lives with total freedom and neurotically blame others for their failures and lost dreams.[11]

The ability to claim ownership for her decisions, her mistakes, and her successes is an important factor in the development of Grand Prix Winner's strong self-confidence, independence, and self-esteem which allow her to be a big risk taker. All these factors influence her ability to succeed.

The prevailing theories about a woman's ability to succeed include socialization and the "glass ceiling." Both theories point out general factors that limit a woman's potential in her profession, but do not deal with the various psychological stages that might alter such potential.

Even more than her professional and technical proficiency, a woman's level of self-confidence, self-esteem, and ability to take responsibility for her own decisions determine her ability to succeed in organizational terms—power, top management, key player.

Socialization. We have already discussed portions of socialization and used examples from observations and experiments which have been conducted by sociologists during the past 30 years. Essentially, the findings have been consistent and point to the strong influence of society's perception and expectations of male and female behavior. From childhood boys and girls seem to be subjected to unspoken value systems which are gender-specific and to approval and disapproval of behavior based on sex.

The tradition of "sugar and spice and everything nice" and "frogs and snails and puppy dogs' tails" has molded women and men for generations, and in the process, sex stereotyped behavior and values became a strong part of American society and its legacy. Men and women dutifully assumed the roles which society has designated: women are expected to be nurturing, expressive, and supportive, while men are concerned with leadership, power, and influences.

Despite the feminist movement, these strong behavioral traits have continued to play a big part in restricting the development of self-esteem and professional success for women.

The "glass ceiling" theory suggests that women cannot move beyond middle management because of invisible organizational discrimination towards them. Morrison, White, and Van Velsor wrote that organizations still have stereotyped views of women and their abilities and reliability. Consequently, the authors concluded that they expect to see no more than a handful of women reach the senior management level of Fortune 100-sized corporations within the next two decades, because the barriers that keep women out of senior management today will remain.[12]

But even more important than the external obstacles that prevent women from reaching the top are the internal psychological barriers women impose on themselves. Research has shown that women are as intellectually capable of tackling any field as men. The differences in their verbal and math performances was attributed to social expectations and pressures during adolescence. The gap is now essentially closed, and both sexes perform equally well in all subjects. So there is no difference in intellectual ability to prevent women from achieving the same level of success as men—if they want to.

The will to succeed is the big "if." Interviews with and studies of women show definitively that women subconsciously inhibit their own professional potential and growth. They have been socialized to believe that men are more relevant than women, to need approval from others, and to fear confrontation and risk. As a result, women defer to men, turn down promotions if they will become isolated from their friends, and take only those responsibilities that they can perform with minimum mistakes and risks. This attitude sets the boundaries for a woman and severely limits her options. It also places her fate in the hands of others, since she is unwilling to take risks and throw caution to the winds.

In her article "Male-Female Interpersonal Styles in All Male, All Female, and Mixed Groups," Elizabeth Aries points out that a person's sex does have a great effect on his/her interactive style. For example, high-dominance women were found to assume leadership over low-dominance women but not over low-dominance men. And, as we pointed out earlier, women are less confident about their views in the presence of men and are more likely to agree with men's opinions.

In mixed groups men initiated and received more interaction than females. Women spoke less in mixed groups and initiated less than one-third of the total interaction. They showed more inhibitions than men. Aries concluded that mixed groups created greater humanness among men and a greater inhibition among women.[13] We see that cultural stereotypes and behavioral patterns are held by men as well as women. As we have said before, by complying with social expectations and roles women limit themselves to be noncompetitive and to be defined by their sexuality rather than by their capabilities.

Rosabeth Moss Kanter, an expert on organizational dynamics, has stated repeatedly that professional women often impose distance and anonymity on themselves when they work in male-dominated groups. In addition, they adopt obsequious behavior by disappearing into the organizational woodwork. They neither assert themselves nor take credit for their own successes and accomplishments.[14]

Grand Prix Winners, on the other hand, feel confidant about whom they are and what they have achieved. Neither Dot nor Joanne apologizes for her success. Neither attributes her accomplishments to luck. Both take full responsibility for their careers and lives. They are the antitheses of the passive, neurotic woman who Karen Horney says chooses predictability over self-actualization and always blames others for her unsatisfactory life.

Grand Prix Winners are willing to make decisions for their own lives, and if those decisions are wrong, they admit their mistakes and try again. Grand Prix Winners don't feel personally jeopardized by setbacks. Perhaps it is because Grand Prix Winners were raised with many nontraditional values and have always felt that the idea of female "inferiority" and stereotypes did not apply to them.

Interpersonal skills and management style. For most executives the ability to deal effectively with co-workers is a learned skill. A few people have a natural intuitive style without formal training, but most of us have to learn by trial and many mistakes. Our personalities and our level of confidence mold the way we interact with people in work and social settings. Whether a person is shy or outgoing, aggressive or passive, goal-oriented or people-oriented all have a great influence on the outcome of that person's life. These traits help form not only personal style but also the ability to realize personal ambitions.

As we have asserted throughout the book, women have grown up with a tradition of being self-effacing, friendly and helpful, and nonthreatening. These nice human traits go a long way in family and social settings. However, they don't translate as well in business and professional environments. Instead they often wave a flag that women with these traits are willing to become the workhorses and mother images for the company. And that is exactly what happens to them. They stagnate in routine jobs, are never given appropriate credit for their ideas or work, and are the sympathetic shoulder on which everybody leans.

As more women entered professions as a lifetime career in the last 25 years, women who were serious about upward mobility began to acquire the personal and management styles of men in the company. Suddenly women were wearing blue and gray suits which could be distinguished from men's suits only by the substitution of a skirt for a pair of pants. Women downplayed their femininity and emphasized their toughness and ability to play "hard ball."

Grand Prix Winners have quite a different style. They aren't too traditionally feminine or too ardently feminist and have a generally low-key interpersonal management style. None of the Grand Prix Winners could identify the reasons for this style, but it could be that they have a firm sense of self-esteem and great confidence in their professional abilities and goals. They convey the feeling that they are comfortable with themselves and don't have the need to posture about their importance or toughness.

Grand Prix Winners were trained in management techniques. They are quite adept at planning, goal setting, and problem solving. They make efficient use of time and are decisive. They know how to create cooperative teams with co-workers and subordinates and by all accounts are excellent managers.

Joanne summed it up, "I think that my ability to manage well without emulating the tough male role model is the result of my being raised nontraditionally. I have been able to develop a better sense of myself as a person and as a woman. I grew up thinking that females are every bit as relevant and competent as males, so I never had internal pressures to be anybody but myself.

"Many women at the top built management skills by doing it. Some didn't know about business school models of goal orientation versus people orientation, high energy versus low energy. We got experience in all those areas of planning, goal setting, budgeting and team building by hands-on experience. We see how our method works and fails and then correct it or improve on it. There isn't much academic hocus-pocus to the process."

The style of Grand Prix Winners is a combination of experience and training in management. They all have been schooled in important aspects of running an organization. Dot and Joanne, for example, received leadership training at the Center for Creative Leadership while they were involved with the League of Women Voters. Dot was then trained by Knight Ridder for three years in all aspects of running a newspaper.

Networks. Networks are indispensable for both men and women. They are sources of information and support. They provide a place to exchange ideas and seek advice. They represent a group of mutually supportive and trusted people who can vent their vulnerabilities and frustrations to each other. A network is a place where you can openly express opinions and emotions without being judged.

In order for a network to work well, it has to be composed of people who are not threatened by each other and who genuinely want to support and be supported. Queen Bees can never network; they could go through the motions of supporting women but would then double-cross them.

Grand Prix Winners are committed to helping other women move ahead. Because they have the success and self-confidence few women have, they can and do support women because they are fully aware of the growth limitations women encounter in organizations and in their own minds.

"We provide enrichment for each other, and through our collective dedication to helping women, maybe we can expand people's horizons. We are in positions to do that—through funding programs, through influencing public opinion," Joanne says. According to Judith Bardwick, Barbara Bunker, and Edith Seashore, women have a greater need than men to have networks. Emotional support is a necessary condition for many women to take risks—not because they are fragile but because they are outside the male network.

Women in networks form close personal links with each other. They discuss not only professional issues but also personal feelings. They become confidantes for each other and use their interpersonal skills to help their friends work through sticky personal situations.

This ability distinguishes women's networks from men's. As Bunker and Seashore point out, men think of friendship in terms of sports and recreation. They never reveal their feelings to these friends, only to lovers.[15] Aries also found that men emphasize competition and leadership with other men, while women generally develop ways to express concern with other women.[16]

Networks, then, provide women with moral and real support and are invaluable in helping women to help each other. But only those who are high achievers, like Grand Prix Winners, can reach out to others without feeling jeopardized. And Grand Prix Winners could not have gotten where they are without networks.

Power. Grand Prix Winners have real power. They have achieved it against the grain of our organizational success patterns. They control policy, budgets, information, and other resources. They influence goals, directions, and public opinion. They make far-reaching decisions and take responsibility for those decisions. Grand Prix Winners not only can handle their position, they also are extremely effective. They have competed and taken risks in the mainstream and excelled.

Unlike women in other stages of development, Grand Prix Winners love to be competitive and don't take failures personally. Their nontraditional background provided an advantage over more conventional women. Grand Prix Winners did not have to learn new behaviors to succeed professionally because they never behaved like or had the values of the traditional American woman.

As Joanne said, "From the time I was a young girl, my parents encouraged me to be a leader to end social injustices. My participation in sports built confidence in my physical abilities. Going to a women's college opened up leadership opportunities, and working in ward politics underscored the importance of having representation and power."

"I enjoyed being president of the foundation. It brings together many things I've done in my life. When this position came along, I was ready. I love the challenge and the potential to chart new directions. I love the ambiguity, the problem solving, the responsibility. I delegate a great deal and try to save time and energy for important issues."

Dot also enjoys power. "With the newspaper, as with the League of Women Voters, I enjoy the power. It puts me in a position to advocate public interest issues, to respond to social and political problems, and to help the community move toward new directions and achievements."

Grand Prix Winners relish power and the opportunities for change and influence which accompany that power. They don't feel strained by it or alienated from others because of it. They don't apologize for having achieved it along with their other successes. Unlike Superwoman, for example, Grand Prix Winners don't shrink from challenges, promotion, or the limelight. They know their capabilities and take full credit for their achievements. They do not attribute their successes to chance or hard work as Superwomen do.

Ruth Holcomb observed in her book *Women Making It* that economic, social, and psychological forces have worked to discourage women from rebelling. Instead, they were rewarded for conformity.[17] Even men who promote equality for women have not been able to ignore that part of their programming which makes them see women as mothers, wives, daughters—but not leaders.

The women's movement set the stage for women to take responsibility for their own lives and to make things happen. Grand Prix winners learned early that they had to become team players. When they lost, they started looking for another game. They were always looking ahead for the next challenge. The result of successive wins is real power. And by winning they get to a position where they can achieve increasingly important goals.

Grand Prix Winners' goals are clear and realizable. While women in other stages only dream, Grand Prix Winners dream, plan and execute. They know where they want to go and how to get there. They pick up opportunities and signals for moving ahead and use their experience and connections to influence the outcomes.

But Grand Prix Winners do not necessarily become role models for all other women. The power of tradition is stronger than the accomplishments and power of Grand Prix Winners. So Grand Prix Winners are often viewed with ambivalence by other women.

Judith Bardwick noted in her article "Some Notes about Power Relationships between Women" that other women often hate women who are powerful. The reason is that powerful women make it hard for powerless women to attribute their powerlessness to external forces. The weaker woman feels that the stronger woman is deliberately limiting the weaker woman's chances to get power or to become a leader.

Women in some of the other stages have fragile self-images and are threatened and jealous of Grand Prix Winners.

Bardwick confirms the strength of Grand Prix Winners: "Powerful women seldom experience the lack of power or helplessness. They do not perceive themselves as withholding power from others.[18]

In describing a good role model for other women, Bardwick describes the Grand Prix Winner. "The greatest model is a woman with personal power, confidence, assertive skills, and high achievements. At the same time she conveys empathy, warmth, and caring."[19]

Bunker and Seashore echo Bardwick in their work "Power Collusion, Intimacy." In discussing the various types of power, they assert that legitimate power requires clear decision making, assertiveness, and accountability and that personal power includes the power to influence, the ability to solve hard problems, strength, and energy, as well as sensitivity and warmth.[20]

The theoretical model and reality come together in the Grand Prix Winner. And even though power is a very difficult trait for most women to accommodate because of socialization, Grand Prix Winners assume it without difficulty and regard power as yet another opportunity to achieve their goals.

Most of the studies of the psychological limitations women impose on themselves and their careers draw remarkably similar conclusions and make similar recommendations. Bardwick, Bunker and Seashore, Hennig and Jardim, and Adams, among others, all feel that women suffer conflicts between being high achievers and "real" women. In order to escape from the conflict and "moribund life of a corrupt and decaying social order"[21] by being emotionally manipulated by society, they need to stop emphasizing their mothering and nurturing instincts. Instead, they should develop their abilities to conceptualize, to take charge and credit for their professional and personal lives.

Grand Prix Winners do not have bloated egos about their accomplishments or power. In fact, they take their successes in stride and genuinely support other women in their efforts. Grand Prix Winners are scarce in number, but they willingly serve as mentors for other women and as role models for women who want to get to the top.

The visions, dreams, and success of Grand Prix Winners provide all women with evidence that they can accomplish anything they set their minds to. By using their talents and skills Grand Prix Winners have emerged at the top by persuading others that their points of view and goals are reasonable and achievable. Their unassuming but uncompromisingly firm commitment to change many social and economic systems will become a reality during the course of their lives because they will work hard to achieve those reforms and to modify those systems.

Grand Prix Winners might not all dramatically change the course of history or social systems, but they will definitely leave their small footnote in history. All of them will most certainly have played an important part in helping to build brighter tomorrows for future generations, and all of us will be the beneficiaries of their courage, determination, and accomplishments.

Grand Prix Winners, through cooperation rather than confrontation and through initiative rather than reaction, proved that women need not voluntarily submit their lives for others to dictate. They were not confined by the traditional roles that have often provided women with excuses for failures and created barriers to their success. They showed what levels of personal and professional success women can have if they will not capitulate to the barriers so common to women. The message Grand Prix Winners convey to all women is to dare greatly. It is the message of encouragement to all women to become vital, relevant human beings.

CONCLUSION

All new systems, whether political, economic, or social, bring reactions of anxiety and anticipation, reluctance and excitement, inertia and energy. The great unknown of the women's movement—of what changes the women's movement would bring to the individual woman, to women in general, to the family, and to the traditional social fabric--seemed to signal a great upheaval of values and social systems at the same time that it signaled the shedding of old limitations and the creation of new opportunities and hope. The unpredictable future of the women's movement and the inevitable changes it would bring were at once unsettling and encouraging. There is no doubt that during the past 30 years the feminist movement has raised both the American public's consciousness level and women's aspirations. We women were told to reach for as full a measure of self-actualization as we wanted: we no longer had to be prisoners of the traditions and myths of womanhood. We no longer had to be the sole proprietors of nurturing and compassion. We no longer had to be passive recipients of actions beyond our control. We could in fact take charge of our own destinies.

However, the constant reassuring encouragement and advice on every conceivable problem we might encounter seemed only to increase the internal conflicts for a substantial number of women. As we have discussed in this book, the feminist movement created seductive and real pressures to conform to a new value system. To do less would be to surrender potential and autonomy. So tens of millions of women dashed forward to be counted. And although they were highly trained and intelligent, many millions of women adopted the role of the modern woman, thinking that a miraculous transformation would take place. All the past encumbrances of socialization and traditional expectation would be replaced by a new, liberated mindset and value system. Everyone—both men and women—would realize that the American woman no longer wanted to be a fairy tale princess but a dynamic, relevant person in her own right.

The tantalizing new social framework of women's liberation became a much-needed alternative to the traditional role women had had for generations. Today's American woman now has greater opportunities, higher ambitions, and greater achievements than her mother and grandmother had. The modern woman is free to take social and professional initiatives and can reach for and attain the stars if she wants to.

There is not doubt that American society has been altered forever by the women's movement, and although many wax poetic and nostalgic about the good old days of motherhood and apple pie, the clock can never be turned back. Just as the Industrial Revolution created new economic and manufacturing systems, so, too, the women's movement is an important part of a social revolution.

The movement has not been without vocal and active resistance during the last three decades. To a large extent, that resistance has been based on the fear of taking responsibility for one's own future and destiny and the fear of the dissolution of those social traditions that provided women with predictable roles. As we have discussed in this book, most women grew up with strong conventional values and traditions that have been part of the proud legacy of American families for generations. The traits and behavior of Hearth Tenders, Superwomen, Beyond Superwomen or Boat Rockers are a deeply ingrained part of our social structure and have provided comfort and emotional security to them. That clear definition of a woman's place in the family and in society made her life and life path clear and uncontroversial. She does not have to make hard value or personal decisions if she subscribes to the predetermined fate of the American tradition.

But the quirks of personality and personal ambition play a role in influencing these women even if they subconsciously and passively resist the women's movement. The existence of the different stages of psychological development attest to that. These traditional women with conventional values fall into particular categories and often straddle them without knowing where they are or how they got there. And many remain in one state of psychological development for the rest of their lives and survive.

But if the American woman wants to grow, flourish, and lead a fulfilling life, she must make a concerted effort to develop psychologically as well as professionally and personally. Risks are inherent in the process, and losses and pain are part of that process. The price is often very high: hostility from men and other women who feel jealous or threatened, backstabbing, isolation, and discrimination.

On the other hand, the American woman can find reasonable satisfaction in her status quo. In order to achieve that, she must at least know where she is, what that status entails, and consciously decide to be there. She will then have selected her life direction rather than be in the position of having it selected for her.

There is no perfect stage for the American woman as a gender because levels of psychological, emotional, and intellectual needs vary as much among women as they do among men. The most anyone can work toward is a stage where she feels most comfortable. If the American woman can achieve that, she will have gone far toward eliminating the guilt, depression, and anxiety she has for not fulfilling society's expectation of being the perfect American woman.

NOTES

Preface

1. Betty Friedan,*The Feminine Mystique*, New York: Norton, 1963.

Stage I: Hearth Tender

1. "Poor little me" is one of the games women play to avoid asserting themselves. This and other manipulations are defined and discussed in *The New Assertive Woman* by Lynn Bloom, Karen Coburn, and Jean Pearlman, New York: Delacort Press, 1975.
2. Carol Gilligan, *In a Different Voice*, Cambridge: Harvard University Press, 1982.
3. Caryl Rivers, Rosalind Barnett, Grace Baruch, *Beyond Sugar and Spice: How Women Grow, Learn and Thrive*, New York: Putnam, 1979.
4. Carol S. Dweck and Ellen S. Bush, "Sex Differences in Learned Helplessness: Differential Debilitation with Peer and Adult Evaluators," *Developmental Psychology*, 1976, 12, 149.
5. I. Broverman, et. al., "Sex Role Stereotypes: A Current Appraisal," *Journal of Social Issues*, 1972, pp. 28, 59-78.
6. Sandra L. Bem, "The Measurement of Psychological Androgyny," *Journal of Consulting and Clinical Psychology*, 1974, pp. 42, 155-62.
7. Sandra L. Bem, "Probing the Promise of Androgyny," *The Psychology of Women*, New Haven: Yale University Press, 1987, pp. 206-225.
8. Helen DeRosis, *Woman and Anxiety*, New York: Delta, 1979.
9. Interestingly, Sandra Bem found that these feminine women were actually less nurturing than androgynous men and androgynous women. These feminine women were more inhibited when social action was not prescribed by society. They are insufficiently assertive to act out nurturing when they must take responsibility for initiating and sustaining interaction.
10. Anne Wilson Schaef, *Women's Reality*, Minneapolis: Winston Press, 1981.

11. Ibid., p. 32.
12. DeRosis, *Women and Anxiety*, 151-54.
13. Ibid., pp. 116-117.
14. Ibid., pp. 49-72, 87.

Stage II: Superwoman

1. Judith Bardwick and Elizabeth Douvan, "Ambivalence: The Socialization of Women," in Vivian Gornick and Barbara K. Moran (eds.), *Women in Sexist Society: Studies in Power and Powerlessness*, New York: New American Library, pp. 226-227.
2. Ibid., p. 228.
3. Lucy Komisar, "The Image of Women in Advertising," in Gornick and Moran, *Women in Sexist Society*, p. 310.
4. Ibid., p. 311.
5. Phyllis Braiker, *The Type E Woman*, New York: Dodd, Mead and Co., 1986, p. 49.
6. Karen Horney, *Self Analysis*, New York: W.W. Norton and Co., 1942, p. 51.
7. Ibid., pp. 72-73.
8. Ibid., pp. 75-82.
9. Ibid., p. 51.
10. Nancy Chodorow, "Being and Doing: A Cross Cultural Examination of the Socialization of Males and Females," in Gornick and Moran, *Women in Sexist Society*, pp. 260-73.
11. Karen Horney, "The Dread of Women," *International Journal of Psychoanalysis* 13 (1932): 359.
12. Sandra L. Bem, "Probing the Promise of Androgyny," *The Psychology of Women*, New Haven: Yale University Press, 1987, pp. 208-221.
13. Bardwick and Douvan, "Ambivalence," p. 227.
14. Alice Wilson Schaef, *Women's Reality*, Minneapolis: Winston Press, 1981, p. 24-29.
15. Bardwick and Douvan, "Ambivalence," p. 227.
16. Matina S. Horner, "Sex Differences in Achievement Motivation and Performance in Competitive and Non-competitive Situations," (doctoral dissertation. University of Michigan, 1968). Dissertation Abstracts International, 1969, 30, 407 B.
17. Michelle A. Paludi, "Psychometric Properties and Underlying Assumptions of Four Objective Measures of FOS," *The Psychology of Women*, 1987, pp. 183-200.
18. Helen A. DeRosis, *Women and Anxiety*, New York: Delacorte Press, 1981, p. 72.
19. Ibid., pp. 37-46.
20. Phyllis Chesler, "Patient and Patriarch: Woman in the Psychotherapeutic Relationship," in Gornick and Moran, *Women in Sexist Society*, 370-373.

21. Margaret Adams, "The Compassion Trap," *Women in Sexist Society*, p. 559.
22. Ibid., p. 563.

Stage II: Beyond Superwoman

1. Rosabeth M. Kanter, *Men and Women of the Corporation*, New York: Basic Books, 1977.
2. M. Z. Rosaldo, "Women Culture and Society: A Theoretical Overview," M. Z. Rosaldo and E. L. Lamphere (eds). *Women Culture and Society*, Stanford: Stanford University Press, 1974, pp. 1-16.
3. Paul Johnson, "Women and Power: Toward a Theory of Effectiveness," *The Journal of Social Issues*, 1976, 32(3), pp. 99-110.
4. Nine L. Colwill, *The New Partnership*, Palo Alto: Mayfield, 1982, p. 97.
5. Gunnar Myrdal, *An American Dilemma: The Negro Problem and Modern Democracy*, New York: Harper & Row, 1944.
6. Paul Johnson, "Social Power and Sex Role Stereotyping," University of California, Los Angeles, 1974.
7. Colwill, *Partnership*, p. 99.
8. Established in 1959 by French and Raven, the six bases of social power are still recognized and used by social researchers and psychologists.
9. Kanter, *Men and Women*.
10. Colwill, *Partnership*, p. 102.
11. Benson Rosen and T. H. Jerdee, "Effects of Employee's Sex and Threatening Versus Pleading Appeals on Managerial Evaluation of Grievances," *Journal of Applied Psychology*, 1975, 60 (4), pp. 442-445.
12. Colwill, *Partnership*, p. 104.
13. Kanter, *Men and Women*,
14. M. E. P. Seligman, *Helplessness: On Depression, Development and Death*, San Francisco: Freeman, 1975.
15. Kanter, *Men and Women*, pp. 377-80.
16. Rollo May, *Power and Innocence*, New York: W. W. Norton, 1972.

Stage IV: Boat Rocker

1. David Campbell, *If You Don't Know Where You Are Going, You'll Probably End Up Somewhere Else*. Allen: Argus Communication, 1974, p. 30.
2. Martha McKay, Lecture to Center for Women in Educational Leadership, University of North Carolina, Chapel Hill, 1980.
3. Robert Alberti and Michael Emmons, *Your Perfect Right*, San Luis Obispo: Impact Publishers, 1970.
4. For reference, four levels of self-esteem have been identified: no self-esteem, minimal or psuedo self-esteem, task-specific self-esteem, and true or overall self-esteem.

5. See Appendix B for a self-esteem evaluation. It will provide you with an indication of your own level of self-esteem.
6. Nathaniel Branden, *The Psychology of Self Esteem*, New York: Nash Publishing Company, 1969, p. 119.
7. Helen DeRosis, *The Book of Hope: How Women Can Overcome Depression*, New York: MacMillan, 1981.

Stage V: Grand Prix Winner

1. Ruth Holcomb, *Women Making It*, New York: Ballentine, 1979, pp. 55-65.
2. Margaret Hennig and Anne Jardim, *The Managerial Woman*, New York: Simon & Schuster, 1976.
3. Rosabeth M. Kanter, "Women in Organizations: Sex Roles, Group Dynamics and Change Strategies," *Beyond Sex Roles*, New York: West, 1977, pp. 376-77.
4. Hennig and Jardim, *Women*, pp. 33-34.
5. Elizabeth Aries, "Male-Femal Interpersonal Styles in All Male, All Female and Mixed Groups," *Beyond Sex Roles*, New York: West, 1977, pp. 292-99.
6. Karen Horney, *Our Inner Conflicts*, New York: W.W. Norton & Company, 1945, pp. 146-55.
7. Hennig and Jardim, *Women*, pp. 90-178.
8. Horney, *Conflicts*, pp. 26-32.
9. Hennig and Jardim, *Women*, p. 63.
10. Horney, *Conflicts*, pp. 12, 156-60.
11. Ibid., pp. 26-32.
12. Ann Morrison, Randall White and Ellen Van Velsor, *Breaking The Glass Ceiling: Can Women Reach the Top of America's Largest Corporations?*, Reading: Addison-Wesley, 1987.
13. Aries, "Male-Female," pp. 295-297.
14. Kanter, "Women in Organizations," p. 376.
15. Barbara Bunker and Edith Seashore, "Power, Collusion, Intimacy—Sexuality Support: Breaking the Sex-Role Stereotypes in Social and Organization Settings," *Beyond Sex Roles*, New York: West, 1977, p. 362.
16. Aries, "Male-Female," p. 296.
17. Holcomb, *Making It*, p. 37.
18. Judith Bardwick, "Some Notes about Power Relationships Between Women," *Beyond Sex Roles*, New York: West, 1977, p. 328.
19. Ibid., p. 334.
20. Bunker and Seashore, "Power," pp. 358-61.
21. Margaret Adams, "The Compassion Trap," in Vivian Gornick and Barbara J. Moran (eds.), *Women in Sexist Society: Studies in Power and Powerlessness*, New York: New American Library, 1971, p. 576.

Appendix A

Assertiveness

More and more American Women are beginning to realize through experience that their natural talents and mastery of technical knowledge are merely the minimum requirements to become professionals with promise and potential. They have personally encountered and felt the painful contradiction of the widely touted national credo that vitality, creativity, hard work, and Yankee ingenuity always bring success. They have met obstacles within organizations and struggled with conflicts within their minds that have prevented them from achieving the level of success they set for themselves. In addition, many have been disappointed by the rich and noble promises inherent in the women's movement. Many doors have been opened, but almost nobody has been there to guide these women after they got in. They have, for the most part, been on their own. The prism that once represented brighter dreams and boundless pursuits has, through time and experience, developed more sober and pejorative reflections.

Wiser and more realistic, these women now feel that their future and success will be affected as much by their interpersonal skills and understanding of organizational politics as they are by their track record and technical proficiency.

Assertiveness is probably one of the most valuable skills all of us should have. It focuses on psychological and emotional honesty, spontaneity, and respect for ourselves and others. By honestly acknowledging our real thoughts and feelings, and our acutal strengths and weaknesses, we free ourselves from irrational ideas, imagined scripts, and uneasy self consciousness anchored in insecurity. With an honest assessment and acceptance of ourselves and our thoughts, we become more relaxed mentally and emotionally, more able to take our mistakes in stride, and more willing to be open in our dealings with others.

Spontaneity also strengthens our psychological and emotional health through prompt recognition and resolution of situations and feelings; it helps to eliminate suppressed emotions that can often built to a point of explosion or severe illness. Pent-up negative feelings are especially common among women as we have discussed earlier.

And respect for ourselves and others, which develops as we acknowledge and accept our basic rights as human beings, provides us with a stronger appreciation for our own quirks and assets and those of others.

Together these major components of assertiveness provide us opportunities for an improved progression in both our private lives and professional work. However, because most women have been socialized to behave nonassertively, assertiveness in concept and implementation may seem alien and almost masculine at first. Learning how to be assertive, how to take risks, how to deal with power will all require a great deal of effort. But with an open mind and practice, women can master these crucial interpersonal skills and weave them effortlessly into their existing styles.

Nature of Assertiveness. Judging from the endless number of paperback books on assertiveness training that are on the market, it appears that we Americans are very taken by the idea of self improvement, looking out for "Number One," and pulling our own strings. And they are right. There is nothing more important in an individual's life than the feeling of self worth, confidence, and respect.

I'd like to begin the discussion of the nature of assertiveness by telling you a story about some top officials in a large corporation. This story illustrates the importance of assertiveness training for people at all levels in an organization.

A senior manager was suspicious and authoritarian toward the people who worked for him. He wanted to do the entire job himself because he did not trust the judgment of the managers who reported to him. Even though the managers officially had major responsibilities and authority, the senior manager never delegated anything of importance to them; he never asked them for their input, analyses, or advice. This senior manager held the reins of leadership so tightly that his subordinates were both intimidated and terrorized by him. He made sure that his managers had no real responsibilities or authority.

As in all conditioned and survival responses, these managers learned that they were punished if they contradicted the senior manager, so they quickly became rubber stamps for all his ideas and projects even when they knew he had made wrong decisions.

The senior manager did not seek out or solicit the truth—the facts—so he became isolated. Because the managers feared for their jobs, they remained silent as the corporation's profits steadily declined. The senior manager lost his job; he never knew what hit him. Had the senior manager been assertive, he would have encouraged open and honest discussion. Had the employees been assertive, they would have found a way to express the truth in a way the senior manager could accept. Situations like this are taking place all over the country, and it's deeply affecting the ability of our institutions and organizations to function well.

If an institution can function with feedback that is close to the truth—then it can succeed. But what is happening today is that there is so much nonassertiveness in our organizations that the truth is often the last thing people look for. People are so intent on being team players to ensure their job security, they often are swept up by the organization's expectations. They may not even be aware of they behave. They think they behave one way—but they actually are behaving in a manner and projecting an image that are completely different. We all do it to a certain extent.

We see this principle operating at even the highest levels of government and industry. People just don't know how they're coming across. They don't know when they are acting like nonassertive doormats—or like aggressive and hostile bullies. People tend to be, in effect, blind to their own behavior.

I'd like to give you an example of that type of behavior. I was working with a group of women leaders on assertive communication skills—women who needed them quite badly. They told me that they knew all the material to be presented and wanted to hear something new. The attack was, in assertiveness training language, an aggressive outburst by about a dozen members of the group. Their facial expressions and their voices were angry and contemptuous. Their body language was defiant. They said that they had heard this material before and felt too advanced for any further training. They especially did not want to hear the basic concepts again—because they knew how to say "no" and they'd tell anybody off fast; they knew how to do that.

They did not realize that they were modeling rude, obnoxious behavior that would limit them in any job situation anywhere. They also did not recognize that their aggressive behavior was not "advanced" and that they were actually at fairly elementary levels of interpersonal skills.

That is what is meant then when we say people are blind to their behavior. By acting tough and mean these women thought they were advanced. Actually the state they were in was the stage of "imitation of the male." The women dressed like men and were trying to act like them. Because they are not men—this didn't come off too well. The behavior violated the first principle of assertiveness--to communicate one's thoughts and feelings openly and honestly, in a way that respects the rights of others.

As I discuss the different parts of assertiveness, I would like you to begin looking closely at your life and behavior for areas to which you might be blind. For example, are you an aggressive leader—hostile when you and other make mistakes? Are you a passive nonassertive follower—afraid to tell the truth about the organization to people who need to hear it? Do you set up barriers so that you will not be bothered with the truth? If you do any of the above, know that you have a great deal of company.

Assertiveness can actually help you analyze and identify your behavior patters and styles, even those to which you are currently blind. Training allows you to get used to expressing the ideas and emotions you have always kept suppressed. It gives you a chance to look at yourself honestly and non-judgmentally, and provides you an environment to experiment with new behavioral approaches without fear of repercussion.

Human beings are social animals, and we spend our entire lives interacting and communicating with other people. The ability to interact and communicate effectively and satisfactorily with others is called assertiveness. Like any other skill, assertiveness is not something we learn immediately. We learn it a little bit at a time. We polish our skills. We start with easy tasks and work up toward harder ones.

Assertiveness is not inborn; it is not intuitive; it must be learned. Just what is it? Assertiveness is defined as a complex set of verbal and nonverbal behaviors that a person uses honestly and openly to communicate legitimate rights, feelings, needs, opinions, and wishes to others in a way that is adaptive and socially appropriate. It is not malicious, disrespectful, or manipulative.

In other words, individuals have the right to express honestly what they are thinking and feeling to those around them, as long as they do this in a way that preserves the rights of others. Every person has the right to be treated with respect and has the responsibility to treat others equally.

Women were taught to suppress their true feelings from the time they were little girls. Assertiveness training enables women to accept and assert their true feelings, not what they want to feel, or what they think they should feel, but what they actually do feel.

It is important before one begins to assert oneself to concentrate on two main areas: the understanding of one's rights to be assertive and the identification of beliefs that might work to prevent assertive behavior.

Psychologists point out that in addition to creating unnecessary anxiety within the individual, counterproductive beliefs can cause people to punish themselves if they act assertively.

If a woman does not believe that she has the right to express her opinion, she will punish herself by saying, "You shouldn't have done that. You are aggressive. Your friend will never talk to you again. You should have kept quiet."

Most women encounter intense mental anguish when they assume leadership roles. Because women have been discouraged from aspiring to these roles for so long, there is a feeling that "I can't do this. This is too tough. I will lose all my old friends. Nobody will like me if I am the boss." These irrational beliefs continue to be the biggest psychological barrier women impose on themselves.

Before we begin with the discussion of assertiveness, let me reiterate how difficult it will be for many women to become assertive. The generations of socialized gender specific behavior combined with strong sex stereotypes create obstacles to change. To punctuate the point, here are two fictitious advertisements that emphasize our present male/female stereotypes.

WANTED: INSURANCE EXECUTIVE

Competitive, ambitious person with leadership ability needed to head our Investment Division. We want someone who is self-sufficient and dominant. The position requires strong analytical ability. This is the perfect job for an independent, self-reliant individual.

WANTED: INSURANCE EXECUTIVE

Affectionate, childlike person who does not use harsh language needed to head our Investment Division. We want someone who is cheerful and eager to soothe hurt feelings. The position requires gullibility. This is the perfect job for the tender, yielding individual.

Components of Assertivness. Assertiveness conveys a basic message: This is what I think. This is how I feel. The message is stated without dominating, humiliating, or degrading the other person.

Briefly, the major components of assertiveness are:

1. Respect for yourself and others. It does not mean deferring to others simply because they are older, richer, or of higher rank.
2. Directness. Hinting or beating around the bush and acting like someone should know what you want or how you feel is not being assertive.
3. Honesty. Accurately represent your feelings and opinions without putting yourself or others down. It doesn't mean that you should say everything that crosses your mind. Honesty needs to be balanced with appropriateness.
4. Appropriateness. Consider the situation, the timing, the intensity, and your relationship with the other person.

Assertiveness training teaches men and women to acknowledge their feelings and thoughts, to distinguish rational from irrational beliefs about the outcomes of their actions, and to express themselves spontaneously and honestly.

An assertiveness inventory we used at the Center for Women in Educational Leadership at the University of North Carolina is included at the conclusion of this appendix. It may give you some insights about your present level of assertiveness.

Although we have described aggressive and nonassertive behavior earlier in this book, they are summarized here so that assertive behavior may be more clearly defined and understood as it compares with the other two.

Nonassertion. Nonassertion involves ignoring your own feelings and rights. Nonassertive individuals express feelings, ideas, or goals in a very indirect manner. Anger is rarely expressed. Their behavior is excessively people oriented. They are so concerned about being pleasing and nice to everybody, they allow others to trample them and to violate their rights. They are passive, compliant, nice, and avoid conflict at all costs. They are followers, not leaders. They have low self-esteem and spend a great deal of time apologizing. These people rarely achieve their goals.

The behavior of nonassertive people is often viewed by others as ineffective and generates feelings of disgust. People who are nonassertive feel used and resentful because others are treading over their rights. Anger develops but is turned inward on themselves.

Nonassertive behavior can also be manipulative. By acting helpless and dependent, nonassertive people get what they want without asking directly. Women are particularly adept at this.

This is not to say that we must always choose assertion. There may be times when we don't want to be assertive and choose to be nonassertive. But the key word is choice. If you can act assertively even though in certain circumstances you choose not to, you are an assertive person. On the other hand, if you cannot choose for yourself but allow yourself to be pushed into nonassertiveness or pulled into aggressiveness, your life will always be governed by others. And you will never be an effective leader. The choice is yours.

Aggressiveness. Aggressive behavior is insensitive to the feelings and rights of others. Aggressive individuals express their feelings, ideas, or goals, but do so in a very threatening manner. They achieve their goals at the expense of others with little consideration for the rights of others. With aggressive behavior, they don't care about the consequences of their actions. The behavior is excessively task-oriented. They are so concerned with getting the job done that they move ahead, even if it means totally disregarding the rights of others. It is usually done in the name of efficiency and goals. The behavior may manifest itself as super-task-oriented authoritarian perfectionism. People who are subjected to this kind of authoritarian leadership often learn that style of behavior. Aggression may be expressed directly or indirectly through backstabbing remarks or malicious gossip.

Aggressive behavior generally stems from the inability to deal with an overload of hostile feelings. It is propelled by a driving force to achieve one's goals at all costs, even at the expense of others. This type of behavior is rewarded in men and punished in women. People who constantly reach their goals by violating the rights of others may expect rejection or revenge from others in the future. The behavior may generate guilt feelings and feelings of rejection within oneself. The only type of aggressive behavior permitted women is a passive/aggressive behavior—catty, backstabbing, name-calling.

Since women have not been permitted by tradition to express anger, it frequently comes out in indirect forms. Effective leaders need to learn to be direct in their communication for the best results.

Nonassertive/Aggressive Cycle. A typical pattern for individuals is to express a combination of nonassertive and aggressive behaviors in a cycle. These individuals initially refrain from asserting themselves when rights are violated, act nicely, and avoid expressing anger. The anger builds and explodes in an aggressive or passive-aggressive manner. The person feels guilty over the behavior and returns to being nice again. The cycle is then repeated with a return to nonassertive behavior.

Now that we know have discussed the three basic behaviors—assertive, nonassertive, and aggressive—we need to become aware of the ways in which they are communicated to other people.

As in all interpersonal communication, there is a verbal message and a non-verbal message.

Research has shown that our verbal communication accounts for about 25 percent of our total message. The other 75 percent is non-verbal. Non-verbal stimuli greatly affect interpersonal communication. How we say something is more important than what we say. Our gestures, facial expressions, eye contact, clothes and even hairstyle affect our effectiveness with and ability to influence others.

The non-verbal message conveys a sense of nonassertiveness, assertiveness, or aggressiveness. An assertive statement, accompanied by nonassertive non-verbal behavior will come across as a mixed message. If someone is looking away from you, and twisting her hands, an assertive message is lost in the interchange. Likewise, aggressive, non-verbal behavior, such as a demanding tone of voice or a hostile expression will convey malice where none may be intended. It is important that the verbal behavior and the non-verbal behavior be consistent. Laughing and giggling with an angry message confuses the receiver. An excessively soft tone of voice and a gentle, sweet facial expression are inconsistent with a strong, assertive request. The following non-verbal behaviors should be noted.

Eye Contact. When people are nervous, they tend to look up or down. They may stare at the ceiling or at their feet and avoid eye contact. Assertive eye contact means that a person looks the other person in the eye with a look of respect and looks away periodically. Aggressive eye contact would be a hostile glare or a stare that violates the space of the other person. In some cultures, eye contact is inappropriate, and the criterion needs to be adjusted when interacting with those from other cultures. A look of interest and attention shows other people that you respect them and are listening to what they have to say.

Relaxed Posture. It is helpful to maintain a relaxed posture while asserting oneself. If you act in a confident manner with appropriate non-verbal behavior, you will feel more confident. A rigid or tense appearance or a slouch takes away from what you are saying. Female body language sometimes conveys shyness or submissiveness. All should be alert to posture and behaviors that imply inequality.

Nervous Laughter or Joking. This does not refer to appropriate humor. Laughter, however, is frequently used as a cover-up for embarrassment or nervousness. If you begin to laugh or joke nervously, you should try to focus on what needs to be said rather than on the discomfort.

Excessive Unrelated Head, Hand, Body Movements. Some non-verbal behavior detracts from communication. Hand-wringing or running one's hands through ones hair, for example, do not contribute to interaction. These habits are not always conscious; a friend can be asked to give you feedback, or you may observe yourself in a mirror.

In addition to these non-verbal messages, physical characteristics are also very important: height, gender, size of nose, eye color, hair color, physical attractiveness, and the kind of clothes you wear. Studies have shown that tall males are deemed more credible and are paid higher salaries than short males. Women prefer tall men. Men are considered more credible than women.

Individuals with dark hair are thought to be more credible than those with light hair, and people with brown eyes are considered more trustworthy than people with blue eyes.

Even though we like to think that we judge each person on strengths and personality, studies indicate that physical attractiveness and success have a direct correlation.

It is to our advantage to make ourselves as attractive as possible, because it reflects what we are telling the world about how we feel about ourselves, our self esteem, and worth. It is not vanity; it is essential for good communication and success. Effective communication exists when the receiver of a message gives it the meaning the sender intended. Effective communication exists only when there is feedback.

Feedback is very important because it has a great influence on self concept. How people respond to you affects how you feel about yourself. When we learn anything—whether it is tennis, swimming, math, or any skill—one of the secrets of learning the lessons well is to receive *nonevaluative feedback.*

This simply means that there is a no-fault contract with the learner. We recognize that whatever behavior they have learned or not learned is not their fault. Suppose you are a very nonassertive person. Most women would use this opportunity to knock themselves in the head because they would say, "Well, here is something else that I'm just not good at." You will recall that women have been trained culturally to put themselves down. So when we start assertiveness training, we need to recognize that no one is perfectly assertive. We all vary enormously in the skills we have learned and not learned. It is no one's fault, if your mother was nonassertive and taught you to be that way too. This was just the way things happened. We can now learn new skills and unlearn old habits we no longer want. This takes a tremendous amount of work and it usually goes quite slowly. But it works

Rules for Constructive Feedback

1. Use "I" messages in describing your reactions: "I feel...." Don't evaluate the other person's behavior. Don't say, "You're terrible. You did a very, very bad thing." Describe your reactions in a clear, specific way: "I feel extremely hurt, and put down by your remark."
2. Comment in specific terms, on the specific behavior that has occurred. Try not to generalize about the behavior or situation. Such generalization tends to be vague.
3. Don't use the opportunity to ventilate your own needs. Try not to generalize about the behavior or situation; effective communication and feedback demands specificity.
4. Give feedback only when it may be used for constructive change. Feedback on personality traits over which the person has no immediate control is not helpful.
5. Give feedback that is wanted. Check to make certain the receiver will listen.
6. Feedback is most helpful if given immediately following a situation.
7. Ascertain whether the receiver heard your intended message rather than a message the receiver assumes.
8. Remember to ask yourself: "What is my goal?" before an interchange.
9. Limit comments to your perception of non-verbal behavior, voice tone, eye contact, posture and verbal content of the situation you describe. Offer specific examples.

Effective communication cannot take place unless you hear, and you are heard. It is necessary to be aware of yourself at both a feeling and behavioral level and to be aware of what is happening to other group members. This skill involves active listening.

Active listening includes they key ingredients to open, honest, direct, and spontaneous communication. These ingredients happen to be key to effective assertiveness as well.

1. The first factor is the honest expression of feelings. This actually increases a group's effectiveness and productivity.

2. Acknowledgment of the message. Silence is a great block to communication because it is seen as indifference or unwillingness to relate.

3. Supportive behavior
   a. description
   b. problem orientation
   c. spontaneity
   d. empathy
   e. equality
   f. provisionalism

   Unsupportive behavior
   a. evaluation
   b. control
   c. strategy—hidden motives
   d. neutrality—apparent disinterest
   e. superiority—wealth, power, social standing
   f. certainty--dogmatism

4. Restraint from judgment, criticism, lecturing, moralizing, or teaching.

A simple exercise to improve listening is to make a rule that you must not reply to what the other person says until 5 seconds have elapsed after the other person has stopped talking. This achieves two things: (1) It prevents you from interrupting the other person, and (2) it gives you time to think about what the other person said before you reply. This exercise is deceptive; it is much more difficult than it seems.

Effective feedback is both positive and negative

1. It is used to monitor the process. You are free to use the feedback in any way you want or free not to use it at all. It does not provoke defensive behavior.
2. Immediate feedback is more effective than delayed feedback.
3. Accurate interpretation of the message is necessary, if it is to be of any value. Therefore, meanings can be checked by paraphrasing as well as questioning.
4. Be specific rather than general.

5. Feedback should be directed toward the behavior about which the sender can do something rather than toward behavior or elements beyond control.
6. Use constructive rather than destructive comments.
7. Comments should be limited to relevant points and not be overloaded with too much information.

So far we have discussed the differences between aggression, non-assertion and assertion responses. We have talked about verbal and non-verbal communication as they relate to assertion. We have identified the key elements of feedback and active listening. Now what about the basic assertive rights and limits on these rights? Assertive rights must always be based on personal situations, the others in the situation, the possible consequences and appropriate behavior.

Remember that having assertive rights does not give you carte blanche to do anything you want and to act any way you want. There are many assertive rights, but the most important ones are:

1. The right to act in ways that promote your dignity and self respect as long as it doesn't hurt someone else or you.
2. The right to have and express your feelings and opinions.
3. The right to be treated with respect.
4. The right to say no and not feel guilty.
5. The right to change your mind or even be illogical in making decisions.
6. The right to ask for what you want.
7. The right to do less than you are humanly capable of doing.
8. The right to get what you pay for.
9. The right to make mistakes.
10. The right to choose not to assert yourself.
11. The right to feel good about yourself.

Assertiveness Training—
The Need for Experience Assessment

The reader's experience with assertiveness training will be enhanced and more effective, if there is an assessment of the reader's skills before training begins. This is especially important with assertiveness training because assertive behavior deals with direct, honest, and spontaneous expression of wants, needs, feelings, and rights. Since people differ in their ability to express their feelings and opinions, and since they also differ in their ability to deal with other people effectively, it is important that readers determine how they express themselves. The assessment is helpful in meeting the specific needs of the trainee during assertiveness training.

1 = very much discomfort and anxiety
2 = much discomfort and anxiety
3 = moderate discomfort and anxiety
4 = little discomfort and anxiety
5 = no discomfort and anxiety

Assertive Behaviors

_____ 1. Applying for a job.
_____ 2. Asking for a raise.
_____ 3. Returning merchandise to a store.
_____ 4. Expressing an opinion which is different than that of others in a group.
_____ 5. Telling someone good news about yourself.
_____ 6. Commenting about being interrupted before you are finished stating what you have to say.
_____ 7. Attempting to offer solutions at a meeting of high-powered people and experts.
_____ 8. Stating your views to an authority figure.

Body

_____ 1. Entering or leaving a room where many men are present.
_____ 2. Speaking up at meetings.
_____ 3. Speaking in front of a group.
_____ 4. Receiving a compliment about your physical appearance.
_____ 5. Maintaining eye contact, keeping your head upright, and leaning forward in personal conversation.
_____ 6. Being whistled at by or eyed seductively by men.

Mind

_____ 1. Going out with a group of friends when you are the only one without a "date."

_____ 2. Admitting that you don't know anything about some subject.
_____ 3. Telling people that you are afraid and need help.
_____ 4. Using your authority.
_____ 5. Requesting a meeting with a person.
_____ 6. Asking for comments about your performance.
_____ 7. Asking personal questions.
_____ 8. Asking for clarification of a point about which you are confused.
_____ 9. Requesting expected service which you have not received (such as in a restaurant or store).
_____ 10. Quitting a job.
_____ 11. Asking your friend to return an item she borrowed from you.
_____ 12. Continuing to deal with a person who disagrees with you.

Apology

_____ 1. Not apologizing since you feel you are right.
_____ 2. Being expected to apologize by an authority.
_____ 3. Requesting a favor without apologizing.
_____ 4. Asking whether you have offended someone.

Compliments, Criticism, and Rejection

_____ 1. Receiving a compliment by acknowledging that you agree with the compliment.
_____ 2. Complimenting a friend.
_____ 3. Telling a person with whom you are intimately involved when he or she does something that bothers you.
_____ 4. Telling a friend that he or she is talking too much and you're not interested in hearing any more.
_____ 5. Complimenting a person in whom you are romantically interested.
_____ 6. Telling someone you like her or him.
_____ 7. Telling someone that he or she has treated or judged you unfairly.
_____ 8. Discussing with your supervisor his or her criticism of your work.

_____ 9. Receiving a compliment when you know you don't deserve it.
_____ 10. Asking a person who is annoying you in a public place to stop, such as someone who is talks loudly during a movie.

Setting Limits

_____ 1. Refusing to do your friend a favor because you don't feel like it.
_____ 2. Refusing to let your friend borrow your car.
_____ 3. Resisting a salesman who has spent a lot of time showing merchandise.
_____ 4. Turning down an invitation.
_____ 5. Resisting the request of your supervisor.
_____ 6. Turning down a request to borrow money.
_____ 7. Refusing to take minutes during a meeting.

Manipulation

_____ 1. Telling a person that you think he or she is manipulating you.
_____ 2. Responding to a male who has made patronizing remarks about you as a woman.

Sensuality

_____ 1. Telling a prospective lover about your physical attraction to him or her before any such statements are made to you.
_____ 2. Initiating sex with your partner.
_____ 4. Telling your lover/spouse what feels good to you.

Anger

_____ 1. Expressing anger directly and honestly when you feel angry.
_____ 2. Arguing with another person.

Humor

_____ 1. Telling a joke.
_____ 2. Listening to someone tell a story about something embarrassing, but funny, that you have done.

_____ 3. Receiving negative feedback with a sense of humor.

This is not a validated psychological test, but it is helpful to allow yourself to discover in what areas you are assertive. If you have 1s and 2s under certain categories, you might want to give special attention to these groups.

Books on Assertiveness

Alberti, Robert E. and Emmons, Michael L. *Stand Up Speak Out Talk Back: The Key to Self Assertive Behavior.* New York: New American Library, 1971.
———. *Your Perfect Right.* San Luis Obispo: Impact Publishers, 1970.
Bloom, Lynn Z.; Coburn, Karen; and Pearlman, Joan. *The New Assertive Woman.* New York: Delacort Press, 1975.
Bower, Sharon and Bower, Gordon H. *Asserting Yourself.* Reading: Addison-Wesley, 1980.
Butler, Pamela. *Self-Assertion for Women.* San Francisco: Harper & Row, 1976.
Lange, Arthur J. and Jakubowski, Patricia. *Responsible Assertive Behavior.* Champaign, IL: Research Press, 1980.
Martin, Robert A. and Poland, Elizabeth Y. *Learning to Change.* New York: McGraw-Hill, 1980.
Smith, Manuel J. *When I say no, I feel Guilty.* New York: Dial Press, 1975.

APPENDIX B

Self-Esteem Evaluation

Score as follows:
- 0 = untrue
- 1 = somewhat true
- 2 = largely true
- 3 = true

Score   Statement of Present Condition or Action

_____ 1. I usually feel inferior to others.
_____ 2. I normally feel warm and happy toward myself.
_____ 3. I often feel inadequate to handle new situations.
_____ 4. I usually feel warm and friendly toward all I contact.
_____ 5. I habitually condemn myself for my mistakes and shortcomings.
_____ 6. I am free of shame, blame, guilt and remorse.
_____ 7. I have a driving need to prove my worth and excellence.
_____ 8. I have great enjoyment and zest for living.
_____ 9. I am very concerned about what others think and say about me.
_____ 10. I can let others be "wrong" without attempting to correct them.
_____ 11. I have an intense need for recognition and approval.
_____ 12. I am usually free of emotional turmoil, conflict, and frustration.
_____ 13. Losing normally causes me to feel resentful and unworthy.
_____ 14. I usually anticipate new endeavors with quiet confidence.
_____ 15. I am prone to condemn others and often wish them punished.
_____ 16. I normally do my own thinking and make my own decisions.

_____ 17. I often defer to others on account of their ability, wealth, or prestige.
_____ 18. I willingly take responsibility for the consequences of my actions.
_____ 19. I am inclined to exaggerate and lie to maintain a desired image.
_____ 20. I am free to give precedence to my own needs and desires.
_____ 21. I tend to belittle my own talents, possessions, and achievements.
_____ 22. I normally speak up for my own opinions and convictions.
_____ 23. I habitually deny, give alibis, justify, or rationalize my mistakes and defeats.
_____ 24. I am usually poised and comfortable among strangers.
_____ 25. I am very often critical and belittling of others.
_____ 26. I am free to express love, anger, hostility, resentment, joy, etc.
_____ 27. I feel very vulnerable to others' opinions, comments, and attitudes.
_____ 28. I rarely experience jealousy, envy, or suspicion.
_____ 29. I am a "professional people pleaser."
_____ 30. I am not prejudiced toward racial, ethnic, or religious groups.
_____ 31. I am fearful of exposing my "real self."
_____ 32. I am normally friendly, considerate, and generous with others.
_____ 33. I often blame others for my handicaps, problems, and mistakes.
_____ 34. I rarely feel uncomfortable, lonely, and isolated when alone.
_____ 35. I am a compulsive "perfectionist."
_____ 36. I accept compliments and gifts without embarrassment or obligation.
_____ 37. I am often compulsive about eating, smoking, talking, or drinking.
_____ 38. I am appreciative of others' achievements and ideas.
_____ 39. I often shun new endeavors because of fear of mistakes or failure.
_____ 40. I make and keep friends without exerting myself.
_____ 41. I am often embarrassed by the actions of my family or friends.
_____ 42. I readily admit my mistakes, shortcomings, and defeats.

_____ 43. I experience a strong need to defend my acts, opinions, and beliefs.
_____ 44. I take disagreement and refusal without feeling "put down," or rejected.
_____ 45. I have an intense need for confirmation and agreement.
_____ 46. I am eagerly open to new ideas and proposals.
_____ 47. I customarily judge my self-worth by personal comparison with others.
_____ 48. I am free to think any thoughts that come into my mind.
_____ 49. I frequently boast about myself, my possessions, and achievements.
_____ 50. I accept my own authority and do as I, myself, see fit.

Obtaining your Self-Esteem Index

Add the individual scores of all *even* numbered statements (i.e., 2,4,6,8, etc.). From this total subtract the sum of the individual scores of all *odd* numbered statements (i.e., 1,3,5,7, etc.). This net score is your current Self-Esteem Index, or SEI. For example, if the sum of all the individual scores of the even numbered statements were 37 and the sum of all the individual scores of the odd numbered states were 62, your SEI is 37—62, or a minus 25. The possible range of one's SEI is from minus 75 to +75. Do not be concerned about your SEI, no matter how low. Remember your self-esteem simply is what it is, the automatic product of your heritage and total life experience and thus nothing to be ashamed or embarrassed about. It is important, however, that you be honest with yourself in order to obtain as valid a score as possible. Your SEI is simply a reference point for gauging your progress in building self-esteem. Also remember that no matter how low your SEI might be, you can bring it up to any desired value with conscientious effort.

You might find comfort in the fact that lack of sound self-esteem is a universal problem that varies only in degree. It is, however, often so well camouflaged by false fronts and other protective devices that only a trained observer can detect it.

Courtesy of Dr. Vivian Travis.

REFERENCES

Adams, Margaret. "The Compassion Trap," in Vivian Gornick and Barbara K. Moran (eds.), *Women in Sexist Society, Studies in Power and Powerlessness.* New York: New American Library, 1971.
Alberti, Robert E. and Emmons, Michael L. *Stand Up Speak Out Talk Back: The Key to Self-Assertive Behavior.* New York: Simon & Schuster, 1970.
———. *Your Perfect Right.* San Luis Obispo: Impact Publishers, 1970.
Appley, Dee G. "The Changing Place of Work for Women and Men," in Alice G. Sargent (ed.), *Beyond Sex Roles.* New York: West, 1977.
Aries, Elizabeth. "Male-Femal Interpersonal Styles in All Male, All Female and Mixed Groups," in Alice G. Sargent (ed.), *Beyond Sex Roles.* New York: West, 1977.
Bardwick, Judith. "Some Notes About Power Relationships Between Women," in Alice G. Sargent (ed.), *Beyond Sex Roles.* New York: West, 1977.
Bardwick, Judth and Douvan, Elizabeth. "Ambivalence: The Socialization of Women," In Vivian Gornick and Barbara K. Moran (eds.), *Women in Sexist Society, Studies in Power and Powerlessness.* New York: New American Library, 1971.
Bem, Sandra L. "Gender Schema Theory," in Mary Roth Walsh (ed.), *The Psychology of Women: Ongoing Debates.* New Haven: Yale University Press, 1987.
———. "Probing the Promise of Androgyny," in Mary Roth Walsh (ed.), *The Psychology of Women: Ongoing Debates.* New Haven: Yale University Press, 1987.
———. "The Measurement of Psychological Androgyny," *Journal of Consulting and Clinical Pyschology.* 1974.
Bloom, Lynn Z.; Coburn, Karen; and Pearlman, Joan. *The New Assertive Woman.* New York: Delacorte Press, 1975.
Bower, Sharon and Bower, Gordon H. *Asserting Yourself.* Reading: Addison-Wesley, 1980
Braiker, Harriet B. *The Type E Woman.* New York: Dodd Mead and Company, 1986.
Branden, Nathaniel. *The Psychology of Self-Esteem.* New York: Nash Publishing Company, 1969.
Broverman, I; Vogel, S.; Broverman, D; Clarkson, F; and Rosenkrantz, P. "Sex

Role Stereotypes: A Current Appraisal," *Journal of Social Issues*. 1972.
Bunker, Barbara and Seashore, Edith W. "Power, Collusion, Intimacy—Sexuality, Support: Breaking the Sex-Role Stereotypes in Social and Organizational Settings," in Alice G. Sargent (ed.), *Beyond Sex Roles*. New York: West, 1977.
Butler, Pamela E. *Self-Assertion for Women*. San Francisco: Harper & Row, 1976.
Campbell, David. *If I'm in Charge Here Why Is Everybody Laughing?* Greensboro: Center for Creative Leadership, 1984.
———. *If You Don't Know Where You're Going You'll Probably End Up Somewhere Else*. Allen: Argus Communications, 1974.
———. *Take the Road to Creativity and Get Off Your Dead End*. Greensboro: Center for Creative Leadership, 1985.
Chesler, Phyllis. "Patient and Patriarch: Women in the Psychotherapeutic Relationship," in Vivian Gornick and Barbara K. Moran (eds.), *Women in Sexist Society, Studies in Power and Powerlessness*. New York: New American Library, 1971.
Chodorow, Nancy. "Being and Doing: A Cross-Cultural Examination of the Socialization of Males and Females," in Vivian Gornick and Barbara K. Moran (eds.), *Women in Sexist Society, Studies in Power and Powerlessness*. New York: New American Library, 1971.
Colby, Anne and Damon, William. "A View of Gilligan's *In a Different Voice*," in Mary Roth Walsh (ed.), *The Psychology of Women: Ongoing Debates*. New Haven: Yale University Press, 1987.
Colwill, Nina L. *The New Partnership: Men and Women in Organizations*. Palo Alto: Mayfield Publishing Co., 1982.
DeRosis Helen A. *Women and Anxiety*. New York: Delacorte Press, 1979.
DeRosis, Helen A. and Pellegrino, Victoria. *The Book of Hope: How Women Can Overcome Depression*. New York: Macmillan, 1981.
Dowling, Colette. *The Cinderella Complex*. New York: Summit Books, 1981.
Dweck, Carol S. and Bush, Ellen S. "Sex Differences in Learned Helplessness: Differential Debilitation with Peer and Adult Evaluators," *Developmental Psychology*, 1976, 12:147—56.
Eichenbaum, Luise and Orbach, Susie. *Between Women*. New York: Viking Penguin, Inc., 1987.
Fast, Julius. *Body Politics*. New York: Tower Publications, Inc., 1980.
———. *The Body Language of Sex, Power and Aggression*. New York: Jove Publications, Inc., 1977.
French, J.P.R. Jr., and Raven, B. "The Bases of Social Power," in D. Cartwright and A. Zander (eds.), *Group Dynamics*. Evanston: Row, Peterson, 1960.
Friedan, Betty. *The Feminine Mystique*. New York: W.W. Norton & Co., 1963.
———. *The Second Stage*. New York: Summit, 1981.
Friedman, M. and Rosenman, R.H. *Type A Behavior and Your Heart*. Greenwich: Fawcet, 1974.
Gilligan, Carol. *In a Different Voice*. Cambridge: Harvard University Press, 1982.
Goldbert, Herb. *The Hazards of Being Male*. New York: New American Library, 1977.
———. *The New Male*. New York: Morrow, 1979.
Gordon, Thomas. *Leadership Effectiveness Training*. New York: Wyden Books,

1977.
Greiff, Barrie S. and Munter, Preston K. *Tradeoffs: Executive, Family and Organizational Life.* New York: New American Library, 1981.
Harragan, Betty Lehan. *Games Mother Never Taught You: Corporate Gamesmanship for Women.* New York: Warner Books, 1978.
Harris, Thomas A. *I'm OK—You're OK.* New York: Harper & Row, 1967.
Hennig, Margaret and Jardim, Anne. *The Managerial Woman.* New York: Simon & Schuster, 1976.
Holcomb, Ruth. *Women Making It.* New York: Ballentine, 1979.
Horner, Matina S. "A Psychological Barrier to Achievement in Women: The Motive to Avoid Success," 1968. Reprinted in D.C. McClelland and R. S. Steel (eds.), *Motivation Workshops.* New York: General Learning Press, 1972.
———. "Fail: Bright Women," *Psychology Today.* November, 1969.
———. "Sex Differences in Achievement Motivation and Performance in Competitive and Noncompetitive Settings," *Dissertation Abstracts International.* 1969 30 (407B).
———. "Toward an Understanding of Achievement-Related Conflicts in Women," in Mary Roth Walsh (ed.), *The Psychology of Women: Ongoing Debates.* New Haven: Yale University Press, 1987.
Horney, Karen. *Feminine Psychology.* New York: W.W. Norton & Company, 1967.
———. "The Dread of Women." *International Journal of Psychoanalysis.* 13 (1932) : 359.
———. *New Ways in Psychoanalysis.* New York: W.W. Norton & Company, 1939.
———. *Our Inner Conflicts.* W.W. Norton & Company, 1945.
———. *Self Analysis.* New York: W.W. Norton & Company, 1942.
Johnson, Paul. "Social Power and Sex Role Stereotyping," University of California, Los Angeles, 1974.
———. "Women and Power: Toward a Theory of Effectiveness," *The Journal of Social Issues.* 1976, 32(3), pp. 99—110.
Jongeward, Dorothy and Scott, Dru. *Affirmative Action for Women: A Practical Guide for Women and Management.* Reading: Addison-Wesley, 1975.
Kanter, Rosabeth Moss. *Men and Women of the Corporation.* New York: Basic Books, 1977.
———. "Women in Organizations: Sex Roles, Group Dynamics and Change Strategies," in Alice G. Sargent (ed.), *Beyond Sex Roles.* New York: West, 1977.
Kaplan, Robert E.; Drath, Wilfred H.; Kofodimos, Joan R. *High Hurdles: The Challenge of Executive Self-Development..* Greensboro: Center for Creative Leadership, 1985.
Kiley, Dan. *The Peter Pan Syndrome.* New York: Dodd, Mead & Co., 1983.
———. *The Wendy Dilemma.* New York: Arbor House Publishing, 1983.
Komisar, Lucy. "The Image of Woman in Advertising," in Vivian Gornick and Barbara K. Moran (eds.) , *Women in Sexist Society, Studies in Power and Powerlessness.* New York: New American Library, 1971.
Korda, Michael. *Power.* New York: Ballentine Books, 1975.
———. *Success.* New York: Random House, Inc., 1977.
Lange, Arthur J. and Jakubowski, Patricia. *Responsible Assertive Behavior.* Champaing: Research Press, 1980.

Martin, Robert A. and Poland, Elizabeth Y. *Learning to Change.* McGraw-Hill Book Company, 1980.
May, Rollo. *Freedom and Destiny.* New York: W.W. Norton & Company, 1981.
―――. *Power and Innocence.* New York: W.W. Norton & Company, 1972.
McKay, Martha. "Behavioral Knowledge and Skills." Lecture presented to Center for Women in Educational Leadership, University of North Carolina, July 10, 1980.
Meininger, Jut. *Success Through Transactional Analysis.* New York: Grosset & Dunlap, 1973.
Miller, Jean Baker. *Toward a New Psychology of Women.* Boston: Beacon Press, 1976.
Millett, Kate. *Sexual Politics.* New York: Doubleday and Company, 1969.
Molloy, J.T. *Dress for Success.* New York: P.H. Wyden, 1975.
Morrison, Ann; White, Randall; and Van Velsor, Ellen. *Breaking the Glass Ceiling: Can Women Reach the Top of America's Largest Corporations?* Reading: Addison-Wesley, 1987.
Myrdal, Gunnar. *An American Dilemma: The Negro Problem and Modern Democracy.* New York: Harper & Row, 1944.
Paludi, Michelle. "Psychometric Properties and Underlying Assumptions of Four Objective Measrues of FOS," In Mary Roth Walsh (ed.), *The Psychology of Women: Ongoing Debates.* New Haven: Yale University Press, 1987.
Rivers, Caryl; Barnett, Rosalind; Baruch, Grach. *Beyond Sugar and Spice: How Women Grow, Learn, and Thrive.* New York: Putnam, 1979.
―――. *Lifeprints: New Patters of Love and Work for Today's Women.* New York: McGraw-Hill Book Company, 1983.
Rosaldo, M.Z. "Women, Culture and Society: A Theoretical Overview." M.Z. Rosaldo and E. L. Lamphere (eds.), *Woman, Culture and Society.* Stanford: Stanford University Press, 1974, pp. 1—16.
Rosen, B. and Jerdee, T.H. "Effects of Employees' Sex and Threatening Versus Pleading Appeals on Managerial Evaluations of Grievances," *Journal of Applied Psychology,* 1975 60(4), pp. 442—445.
Sax, Saville and Hollander, Sandra. *Reality Games.* New York: Macmillan, 1972.
Scarf, Maggie. *Unfinished Business.* New York: Ballentine Books, 1980.
Schaef, Anne Wilson. *Women's Reality.* Minneapolis: Winston Press, 1981.
Seligman, M.E.P. "Fall in Helplessness," *Psychology Today.* 1973 7(1).
―――. *Helplessmess: On Depression, Development and Death.* San Francisco: Freeman, 1975.
Shaevits, Marjorie Hansen. *The Superwoman Syndrome.* New York: Warner Books, 1984.
Sheehy, Gail. *Passages: Predictable Crises of Adult Life.* New York: E.P. Dutton & Co., 1976.
Smith, Manuel J. *When I Say No, I Feel Guilty.* New York: Dial Press, 1975.
Stewart, Nathaniel. *The Effective Woman Manager.* New York: John Wiley & Sons, 1978.
Trahey, Jane. *On Women and Power.* New York: Rawson Associates Publishers, 1977.

Travis, Vivian. "Assertiveness, Power, Stress Management and Leadership." Lectures presented to Center for Women in Educational Leadership, University of North Carolina, November 10—11, 1980, January 27—28, 1981, April 9—10, 1981, and April 25—26, 1981.

Tresemer, David. "Fear of Success: Popular but Unproven," *Psychology Today*. 1974, 7(10).

———. "The Cumulative Record of Research on 'Fear of Success,' " *Sex Roles: A Journal of Research*, 1976, 2(3).

Viscott, David. *Risking*. New York: Simon & Schuster, 1977.

Weisstein, Naomi. "Psychology Constructs the Female," in Vivian Gornick and Barbara K. Moran (eds.), *Women in Sexist Socitey, Studies in Power and Powerlessness*. New York: New American Library, 1971.

Westkott, Marcia. *The Feminist Legacy of Karen Horney*. New Haven: Yale University Press, 1986.

Whiteside, Robert L. *Face Language*. New York: Frederick Fell Publishers, 1974.

Willett, Roslyn S. "Working in 'a Man's World': The Woman Executive," in Vivian Gornick and Barbara K. Moran (eds.), *Women in Sexist Socitey, Studies in Power and Powerlessness*. New York: New American Library, 1971.

INDEX

Adams, Margaret, 46
Advertising, 23—26
Aggression,
  Characteristics, 93
  Expression of, 31
  In young girls, 23, 31
Anger,
  Curbing, 23
  Inability to express, 30, 44
Anxiety, 44—46, 98, 120
Aries, Elizabeth, 110, 111, 126, 129
Assertiveness,
  Characteristics, 31, 76, 77, 90—92, 93, 94
  Nonassertiveness, 31, 44—45, 92—93

Bardwick, Judith, 22, 31, 35, 38, 129, 131, 132
Barnett, Rosalind, 10
Baruch, Grace, 10
Bem, Sandra, 11—12, 13, 35
Black Widow Spiders, 100—103
Braiker, Phyllis, 29, 31, 33
Branden, Nathaniel, 97, 98
Broverman, I., 11
Bunker, Barbara, 129, 131, 132

Campbell, David, 89
Center for Women in Educational Leadership (CWEL), 75—76, 77, 80, 81, 82

Chesler, Phyllis, 44, 45, 46
Chodorow, Nancy, 34
Cinderella syndrome, 2, 3, 32, 77, 80
Colwill, Nina, 66
Compassion trap, 46, 106
Coping, 27, 43, 44, 49, 56, 52—63, 78, 90, 107, 111, 127

DeRosis, Helen, 13, 16, 17, 19, 44, 46, 98
Denial, 17, 31, 40, 44—45
Dependence
  Compulsive, 32, 34, 38
  Fear of Success, 40—41
  Total dependence on others, 16, 17, 98
  Traditional life, 13, 22, 45
Depression,
  Internalizing, 44
  Poor self-esteem, 16—17, 20
  Self creation, 45—46
  Stress, 33, 93
Douvan, Elizabeth, 22
Dread of Women, 35
Dweck, Carol, 11
Fear of Success (FOS), 26—27, 38—41, 46, 49, 77
French, J.P.R., 64
Gender differences, 10—13, 16, 22—23, 31, 35, 62, 70, 125
Gilligan, Carol, 10
Glass ceiling, 125

Goals, 84, 85—86, 88, 89, 107, 117—118
Guilt, 23—24, 27, 39, 44, 92—93, 97—98

Helplessness, 13—14, 20, 33—34, 45, 66, 68, 92, 119, 131
Hennig, Margaret, 109, 115, 116, 120
Holcombe, Ruth, 107, 114, 130
Horner, Matina, 38, 41
Horney, Karen, 17, 31, 32, 33, 34, 35, 44—45, 111, 114, 119, 124

Image, women's,
 Advertising, 23—24, 25
 Derivative, 45
 Earth mother, 46
 Executive, 34—35
 Of themselves, 17
Independence (See *Self determination*)

Jardim, Anne, 109, 115, 116, 120
Jerdee, T. H., 66
Johnson, Paul, 62

Kanter, Rosabeth Moss, 60, 66, 67, 70, 109, 126
Komisar, Lucy, 23

Leadership,
 Career progress, 109—110
 Components of, 78—79, 113—115
 Hindrance to, 67
 Leadership style, 57—58
 Seeking out, 99
 Variations in women's dominance, 126
Limit boundaries, 14, 27, 31—32, 38—41, 46, 47, 60, 68

Management skills, 90, 99, 114, 115, 118, 127—128
McKay, Martha, 89, 91
Morrison, Anne, 125

Networks, 114, 128—129

Neurosis,
 Compulsive neurotic, 124—125
 Need for approval, 31
 Need for father figure, 33—34

Obstacles,
 Family demands, 50
 Gender, 63—64
 Glass ceiling, 125
 Identified, 79—80
 Internal conflicts, 102, 126
 Lack of recognition, 51
 Organizational, 51, 63
 Not exercising power, 69
 Overcoming, 78, 80—81, 106, 108
 Personal, 52
 Self imposed, 98, 111, 114, 120, 126, 131—132
 Sex discrimination, 53
 To growth, 111
 To leadership, 67—68
 Tradition, 114

Paludi, Michelle, 41
Passivity, 19, 44—45, 89, 98, 108, 109, 119
Penis Envy, 35
Power,
 Bases of, 64
 Comfort with, 60, 62, 80, 84—85
 Competence with, 66—67
 Differences in men and women, 62—64, 66
 Gender domains, 62—63
 Indirect, 62—63
 Interpersonal, 62
 Legitimate, 106, 108, 129—130
 Limited for women, 62—63
 Powerlessness, 36, 63—64, 66
 Psychological well-being, 69
 Resources, 63
 Women hating other women with, 131
Queen bees, 100—103

Risk taker, 67, 69, 94, 107, 114, 119—120

Rivers, Caryl, 10
Rosen, B., 66

Schaef, Anne, 16
Seashore, Edith, 129, 131, 132
Self determination, 26, 49, 60, 69—71, 78—79, 80, 90, 106—109, 115, 118, 126
Self-esteem,
    Affirmation by others, 18—19, 30—31
    Crisis, 98
    Determine ability to succeed, 125
    Development of, 94, 114
    Female,
        Affirmation by others, 13
        Development of, 84—85
        Inferiority, 16, 17
        Low, 16, 17
        Male influence, 34, 35, 36
        No rights, 45
        Parent's choice, 10, 16—17
        Underrate abilities, 10—11
    Healthy, 114
    Lack of, 102, 120
    Levels identified, 138
    Male,
        Dread of women, 35
        Early development, 35
        Establish self, 34—35
        Influence over women, 36—38
        Overestimate of abilities, 11
    Poor self-esteem, 16—17, 20
    Psuedo self-esteem, 97—98
    Self evaluation survey, 156—158
    True self-esteem, 94, 98
Sex discrimination, 53
Sex role (See *Socialization*)
Socialization,
    Beyond sex roles, 69—71
    Compassion trap, 46
    Definition of, 22—23
    Effect on ambition, 114
    Female need for male validation, 13, 16, 34, 36
    Gender-specific behavior, 10—13
    Influence on behavior, 106—107
    Male and female role tendencies, 70, 126
    Male superiority, 14, 15, 34, 35, 125
    Non-traditional, 115, 117
    Obstacles to growth, 111, 127
    Parents' influence, 16, 34—35
    Powerlessness, 19, 34
    Sex role appropriateness, 41, 130
    Stereotyped roles, 22, 41, 49, 68. 124
Stereotype (See *Socialization*)
Stress, 29, 31, 33, 46, 52
Style, personal,
    Influences, 59, 60, 99, 108, 109, 110, 115, 117—118, 120, 125, 127—128
    Low profile, 67—68, 109, 126—127
    Male/female, 70
    Mixed groups, 126
    Participatory, 60
Success,
    Comfort with, 49
    Defined by others, 29
    Denial of, 40
    Guilt, 39
    Sex role appropriateness, 41
    Social rejection, 39
    Unfeminine, 38
    (See also *Fear of Success*)

Traditional Women, 10—13, 15, 16—17, 22—23, 34—35, 38, 43, 44, 46, 47
Travis, Vivian, 68
Tresemer, David, 41

Velsor, Ellen, 125

White, Randall, 125
Women Crushers, 100—103